ROCHFORD'S HOUSE-PLANTS
FOR EVERYONE

Maranta leuconeura erythrophylla

ROCHFORD'S
HOUSE-PLANTS
FOR EVERYONE

Thomas Rochford & Richard Gorer

FABER AND FABER
24 Russell Square
London

First published in 1969
by Faber and Faber Limited
24 Russell Square London WC1
Printed in Great Britain by
Latimer Trend & Co Ltd Plymouth
All rights reserved

SBN: 571 08826 0 **(Cloth Edition)**

SBN: 571 08827 9 **(Paperback Edition)**

CONTENTS

CONTENTS

ILLUSTRATIONS

between pages 80 and 81

CHAPTER I

HOW PLANTS GROW

If you are going to grow house-plants, it is certainly a good idea to have some idea as to how plants grow. Not that we have complete knowledge of that, even in this scientific age, but it is at least possible to give a rather rough and ready description. Then, when we know how a plant grows, we can be on our guard against some mistakes, even though we may make others. Knowledge is not a substitute for experience, but it is certainly a help.

BREATHING

In some ways you can say that plants behave like we do: they eat, drink and breathe but, of course, the way they do this is quite different from the way that we do. Indeed, in the case of breathing, it is completely the opposite. We, like most vertebrates, take oxygen from the atmosphere, burn it up with carbon in our lungs and breathe out carbon dioxide. The plant, on the other hand, takes the carbon dioxide from the atmosphere, combines it with the hydrogen in water (H_2O) to make a hydrocarbon and breathes out oxygen. Since there is not a great deal of oxygen in the atmosphere at any time you can see that, were it not for the plants always producing more oxygen, life would long ago have become extinct as all the oxygen was used up.

However, the analogy cannot be pressed too far. Human

11

beings, like all animals, do not stop breathing while they are alive, but plants tend to breathe only in daylight. That is because light is necessary for the process, known as photosynthesis, by which the plant turns the carbon dioxide and water into hydrocarbons and oxygen. When light is absent the process stops. The substance that causes photosynthesis to take place is chlorophyll, the green colouring matter in plants. Sometimes this is overlaid by cells of another colour, so that we get red- or purple-leaved plants, although the chlorophyll is still there. In some variegated leaves the chlorophyll is absent in parts of the leaf, with the result that these plants tend to grow rather more slowly than those whose leaves are entirely green.

The leaves are covered with pores, known as stomata, through which the carbon dioxide passes in and the oxygen passes out. Most of these are on the underside of the leaf, but there are also some on the surface. If the plant is in a room these pores are liable to become clogged up with dust, and the plant cannot breathe so freely. That is why it is necessary to sponge the leaves of your house-plants from time to time. It is not only that the dust-covered leaves do not look attractive, but also the plant cannot grow so well, and it is because most of these pores are to be found on the underside of the leaf that you are advised to clean both sides.

LIGHT REQUIREMENT

We have said that chlorophyll can only function when there is light, and in the same way light is necessary to induce the plant to produce chlorophyll. If you are forcing bulbs and put them in a dark place, you will find, when you take them out, that the leaves are not green at all, but a sort of ivory colour. However, they do not need to be in the light for very long before they turn green. Without light green plants cannot grow at all. If you visit stalactite caves such as Wookey Hole or the Cheddar Caves you will find that wherever the electric light shines on the rocks, there will be growing ferns and mosses. The rest of the rocks are bare, but as soon as light, even artificial light, is provided then, almost at once, plants start to appear.

The amount of light that a plant requires depends on the conditions to which it is used in the wild state. Most of the house-plants that we grow come from the tropics. This does not necessarily mean that they are used to very hot conditions—there are snow-covered mountains on the Equator—but it does mean that they are used to bright light. This light may often be considerably filtered, as most of the plants grow in forests. But the intensity of light in the tropics, even in the shade, is often equivalent to the light supplied by full sun in our climate. If our rooms have large windows and are bright, we may have to put some house-plants in a rather shady position, but if they are rather dark we must put them in the lightest position we can find.

HUMIDITY

As we have seen, photosynthesis needs light in order to take place, but the plant must also have water. Much of this will be obtained from the soil in which it is growing by the roots, but some will also be absorbed by the leaves. Sometimes the leaves absorb more water than they can manage and breathe, or transpire, some out again but since most tropical plants like a moist atmosphere around their leaves this does not matter. Out of doors the atmosphere will always be moist enough, but in our rooms, especially in winter when fires may be burning, the atmosphere may be too dry for the plants. We can overcome this to a certain extent by putting the plant in a container, such as a bowl, filling the container with peat, moss, or mica powder, and keeping this moist. As we shall see in a minute, it is not always a good thing for the soil in which the plant is growing to be too wet, but with most plants it is

13

necessary for them to have a moist atmosphere, and we can create that artificially with our wet moss or whatever else is being used. The vapour rises from this and surrounds the leaves of the plant. The same effect can be obtained by putting the plant in sealed containers, such as bottle gardens or Wardian cases. Under these circumstances the atmosphere is not affected by the outside temperatures (provided, of course, that they do not fall too low; you can have frost damage in a bottle garden if it gets cold enough) with the result that the plants are always in the same atmosphere. Your problem here is that the soil will remain in the same condition as it was when you planted it so, if it was too wet then, it will never dry out but remain too wet. If it is too dry you can add more water, but if you have too much it is very difficult to get rid of it.

ROOT FUNCTIONS AND REQUIREMENTS

You may be raising your eyebrows here. How, you may ask, can a plant have too much water? Let us see if we can find out. So far we have only been thinking about the leaves of the plant; let us now think for a moment about the roots. The roots do two things for the plant. They anchor it in the ground. They do not always do this successfully and a violent gale will uproot many trees. It is for this reason that very windswept places are often bare of trees. Either they do not grow at all or they grow very close to the ground so that the wind cannot uproot them.

The other function of the roots is to obtain nourishment from the soil. It is not, however, a very large part of the roots that does this. If you grow mustard and cress on a damp flannel, you will find that the roots stick to the flannel, and if you have a lens, or very good eyesight, you will see that what is sticking to the flannel is a mass of very fine hairs that emerge from the main root. It is these root hairs that absorb the nourishment. The remainder of the roots may be regarded as

14

a sort of plumbing system which transports the nourishment that the roots obtain from the soil to the aerial parts of the plants, the stems, leaves and flowers, while, in reverse, the hydrocarbons that the leaves have manufactured are transported down to the roots. The root hairs are only found at the root tips and do not persist for very long; as the root elongates new root hairs are formed and the old ones disappear.

Now, the root hairs need air in which to develop. There is quite a lot of air in the soil, although we should soon suffocate if we were buried. If you could look at soil through a microscope you would see that it is composed of millions of tiny particles, and between these particles is air. If you go lower down, to the sub-soil, you will find that the weight of the top soil has so impacted this, there is practically no air between the particles. You will also find that there are no plant roots down there. As well as inhibiting the growth of roots, this lack of air will also inhibit the existence of the bacteria and microscopic fungi, which inhabit aerated soil and which break down vegetable refuse and other materials so that they are available to the plant roots as food. Most of these cannot survive without air and so the minerals in the sub-soil do not become available to the plant roots, even though the sub-soil might be rich in nutrients. Similarly the worms will not penetrate to parts of the soil where there is no air.

If the soil is super-saturated, many of these living organisms will cease to exist. In the open ground this condition is only normally found in bogs or in waterlogged ground, and many plants will not flourish in these conditions. There are, of course, plants that have adapted themselves to grow in positions that would kill most plants. Marshes have their own particular plants that thrive there and nowhere else, and other plants such as water-lilies and water-crowfoot will grow actually in the water, but the majority of green-leaved plants require soil that is aerated and well-drained. In this sort of soil even days

15

more than the rhododendron dies when it is exposed to frost, but the roots stop functioning.

Also, during winter, when there is not very much daylight, the leaves cannot function for so long. They do function fairly adequately under electric light, so that if you have very warm rooms and plenty of illumination you can keep your plants growing all the year round, if that is what they would be doing in the wild. However, most of us cannot keep our rooms as warm as the plants would like, and therefore we are advised to keep our house-plants on the dry side during the winter, say from November to mid-March. If the roots and leaves are not functioning very much, they will only take a little water from the soil and there is a risk of this becoming sodden if we water as copiously during the winter as in summer. This can cause root rot and ultimately the death of the plant. If the plant gets too dry the leaves droop and it is easy to see, and easy to redress the balance, but if the plant gets too wet, the harm will not be perceptible until it is very advanced, at a time when cure may be difficult or even impossible. Occasionally excessive moisture will cause leaves to droop, but it can easily be seen whether this drooping is caused by excessive water or drought.

WATERING

More plants are lost by drowning than by any other cause. There are a number of reasons why excessive moisture in soil in a confined space can kill a plant and it would be tedious to enumerate them here.

The fact remains that too much water in the soil is worse than too little. That is not to say that you can always keep your plants too dry. They will not die, as they will if kept too wet, but they will not make good growth, the leaves will be small in size and very dark green in colour. Here again the symptoms are visible and the cure is simply to apply more water. The cure will not be instantaneous, as is the case when leaves are wilting through drought, but it will not be long before you start to see results.

Of course, a plant growing in a pot is in a different environment from one growing in the open soil. The roots cannot spread out to the extent that they would if space were available, and water does not evaporate, at the same rate as it would in the open and, moreover, varies according to the type of pot. There is evaporation from the side, as well as from the surface of clay pots, but in the case of plastic pots, which are being used more and more nowadays, there is no evaporation from the sides, so that watering plants in these pots can take place at less frequent intervals. It is necessary, therefore, to have a special soil mixture for these pots from which all surplus moisture will drain rapidly and this rapid drainage is usually obtained by incorporating plenty of fine grit or sharp sand. This helps to keep the compost in the condition gardeners call 'open'. That is to say, the compost does not flatten or 'pan' down into an impacted mass when it is watered.

When you do water a plant, you should soak the whole of the soil in the pot. It is no good giving just a little, which will only water the top half, or even less, of the soil. That would mean that the bottom half would remain dry, and would be of no use to the roots, which would stop developing and the plant would become starved. If a plant has been properly potted there is a space between the soil level and the brim of the pot. The depth of this space depends on the size of the pot. With a 3-inch pot it will be about $\frac{1}{2}$ an inch and with a 5-inch or 6-inch pot it will be an inch or slightly more. If, when you water, you fill the pot to the brim, this should permeate all the soil in the pot as it soaks down. No more watering should then be done, until the plant has used the water that is already there and the soil has become dry again.

The length of time this will take depends on several factors. The main ones will be the vigour of the plant, and the mixture

19

in which it is potted. During the warm growing-season, when plants are making plenty of root and stem growth, they will be using much more water than during the winter, when they are semi-dormant or during the autumn, when growth is completed and is being ripened. Soil mixtures containing a lot of peat or grit tend to dry out quicker than those that contain plenty of loam. Nowadays the emphasis is on soilless mixtures composed nearly entirely of peat and grit, to which nutrients are added, and these will dry out more rapidly than the John Innes composts, which contain a large proportion of good loam. Unfortunately, good loam is becoming increasingly difficult to obtain and we must expect the trend towards soilless mixtures to continue. These do have the advantage of being so quick-draining that it is not easy to overwater plants that are put in them, so, to that extent, they make the growing of house-plants easier.

To summarize then, the plant is a growing organism. In the air it produces leaves which, with the help of light, take the carbon dioxide and water vapour from the atmosphere and, with the aid of the water obtained from the roots, create hydrocarbons and return the surplus oxygen to the atmosphere. Underground it has a root system which anchors it firmly in the soil and which, by means of the root hairs—produced at the tips of the roots—absorbs chemicals or mineral foods to help build up the plant and make it grow.

RATE OF GROWTH

These processes usually go on simultaneously, but not always. If, for example, you take a daffodil bulb, you will find that it makes a large number of roots before any leaves are produced at all, while, at the other end of its growth cycle, the roots will cease growing before the leaves. Similarly, in the case of many house-plants, the roots will start to grow before you see any signs of leaf growth. In this case, however, there are already leaves present and you can only see that the roots are growing by turning the plant out of its pot. The new root tips are white in colour and, if they have reached the edge of the soil ball, are clearly visible. However, as a general rule, root growth will precede stem growth. This makes the restarting of growth in the spring slightly tricky. If you think that the temperature is high enough, you should start applying rather more water in mid-March, but if it is very cold at that time, it is better to wait until the temperature becomes higher. Very few tropical plants will start to grow with the temperature lower than 55°F, although they will survive perfectly happily at much lower temperatures. Some need higher temperatures before they will even start growing. (When we come to list the more easily grown house-plants, we shall be mentioning the kind of temperatures that they require.)

TEMPERATURE

It can be assumed, within reason, that the higher the temperature is, the faster the plants will grow and therefore they will require watering more frequently than when it is cold. If the heat becomes excessive, the plant wilts, however moist the soil may be, because it is losing so much water through its leaves. This does not happen very often, but when it does, the best thing to do is to spray the leaves with cold water; only a very fine spray is required. This will bring the leaves quickly back to their normal, turgid condition. In any case, they will recover as soon as the temperature falls sufficiently. This is not a condition that troubles house-plants much in any case.

On the other hand, if you place a plant on the mantelpiece above a fire or on a shelf above a radiator, you are asking for trouble. Such a position is far too hot, as well as being too dry and dust-laden. You might get a succulent or a cactus to survive in such a position, but no thin-leaved plant will do so. Such places may be suitable during the summer months, but should be avoided in the winter. The shelf above a coal or electric fire is a real death-trap for plants, as the temperature will fluctuate to an excessive degree. Plants that live in deserts are used to violent fluctuations of temperature; in the desert the day temperature may be in the nineties while it may drop to freezing-point at night, but most plants dislike these rapid changes of temperature as much as we ourselves do. House-plants grow more happily in a constant temperature, even one that may be on the low side, than in one that may be deliciously warm at one moment and too cold at the next.

Indeed, plants, unlike almost all other living organisms, grow in two different temperatures. The air temperature, where the leaves and stems are, is almost always at a higher tempera-ture than the soil, where the roots are. If the soil becomes too warm, the plant does not care for it. Again, the air temperature is always changing, while the soil changes its temperature very slowly. That is why you are recommended to use water at about the same temperature as your room. Very cold water, or very hot water, will change the soil temperature far too quickly and affect the roots. Within a few degrees this does not matter generally, but in the case of the African violet it does seem necessary to have your water always at the same temperature to get the best results. When you water the garden from the hose the coldness of the water does not matter, as there is the whole of the soil in the garden and it is warm enough to warm the little water that you are putting on, up to its own tempera-ture, but the small amount of soil in a pot can have its tem-perature lowered considerably, if it is saturated with very cold water. Most plants are sufficiently tolerant to overcome this shift in temperature, but it does give them a check, even if only a momentary one. The African violet, on the other hand, is very sensitive to these temperature changes and will show it by developing unsightly white blotches on its leaves.

As a matter of fact there is always a risk that the soil in a pot in a room may get slightly too warm and this is an additional reason for putting the pot in a bowl of peat or vermiculite. Not only are you thus able to get water vapour around the leaves, but you also give sufficient insulation to prevent the soil from becoming too warm. However, this is only liable to happen in rooms that are kept continuously at a very high temperature and very few of us have the wish to do this, or the money, even if we have the wish. Incidentally, plants that normally have practically no soil roots, such as many of the bromeliads and the peperomias, will not be affected by the temperature of the soil.

All this may make it sound as if growing house-plants is very difficult. This is not so; there are few plants that are easier, but there is a difference between growing a plant adequately and growing it well. To grow your plants well, you do have to take a little extra trouble, and the purpose of this chapter has been to try and give you some idea as to why one is advised to do certain things. If we know that the plants cannot 'breathe' properly when the leaves are covered with dust, we can see the reason for sponging the leaves periodically; if we know that the roots cannot function when the soil is too wet, we will take steps to prevent it happening. In our opinion few things are more fascinating than the mysterious way plants grow, and even the elementary knowledge that we have ourselves and that we have given here, will add to the interest that there is in growing them.

CHAPTER II

THE HOW, WHAT, WHY AND WHERE
OF HOUSE-PLANTS

There are basically two reasons for buying a house-plant: one is that you think the plant is so beautiful that you *must* have it; the other is that you need some plants in a particular position for reasons of interior decoration. Whatever your reason may be, the result is some problems you have to solve.

In the first case, when you bought the plant because you liked it, you have to find out what sort of conditions it requires to grow well (our last chapter is meant to cover all these details). Does it need a warm or a cool room? Light or shade? A very moist atmosphere or can it tolerate a fairly dry one? Will it react to gas or to oil fumes? Although these questions may sound rather alarming, the vast majority of house-plants are grown as house-plants because they are tolerant of a wide range of conditions, and if you can provide the basic require-ments of warmth and atmosphere, the other problems can usually be overcome.

In the second case, you already know the conditions in which the plant or plants are going to be growing and it is simply a matter of running through the plants available, noting all those that seem suitable. Here, of course, the size of the plants may be a consideration. If you want a trough full of low-growing plants, the fact that the situation is ideal for a rubber tree is irrelevant.

24

POSITION

There are very few positions in the house for which it is not possible to find a house-plant that will grow happily. As has been mentioned earlier, if you have a coal, gas, or electric fire, the mantelpiece immediately above this fire should be regarded as unsuitable. Apart from some desert plants, no green plants can tolerate being alternately roasted and chilled. If they are well illuminated, it is just possible that some cacti will survive on a mantelpiece above a fire that is periodically lit, but even so, they will not be happy. Cacti like to be cool and dry in the winter and though they might enjoy a roasting in the summer, they would find it upsetting in the winter. It is far better to keep the mantelpiece clear of plants.

The case of water-filled radiators is slightly different. The heat is not so intense and it is perfectly feasible to grow plants above them, if sensible precautions are taken. For one reason the heat remains fairly constant, which most plants like—it is the violent fluctuations of temperature that upset so many plants. Very often a plant that we are recommended to over-winter in a temperature of 60°F will manage to survive in a constant temperature of 50°F, while it will suffer if the temperature is sometimes 65°F and sometimes 45°F. Of course, there is always a slight fluctuation under natural conditions. Wherever you are, it is probable that the nights will be cooler than the days and if natural warmth makes your rooms warmer in the daytime, there is no cause for worry. A gradual rise or fall in temperature the plant can easily adjust to, it is the sudden change that is liable to disconcert it. If you stand a croton in a cold draught for quite a short period, you will find the leaves starting to drop.

HUMIDITY

However, this is slightly off our present point; let us get back to our radiator. Any shelf placed above this will be in a constant warm temperature, unless you are very capricious about turning your central heating on and off. The features that the plant will dislike will be the fact that the heat is coming from below, so that the soil and the roots will be warmer than the leaves, and the fact that the air will be very dry. This can easily be dealt with. Put your pot in a container of some sort—a flower bowl, a trough, whatever you have available—and fill the intervening space with peat, or vermiculite, or sand. This will insulate the pot and the soil from too much heat coming from below. Now see that this filling substance, whatever it may be, is kept always moist. You will not need to be constantly watering the pot, but if you keep the filling of your container always moist, it will give off enough vapour to keep the leaves in good condition.

As a matter of fact, this treatment of sinking the pot in a container filled with some water-retentive medium can be followed with advantage for practically every house-plant. It is only natural that in winter we like our rooms to be warm and dry, whereas the plants would prefer them to be warm and moist, and by giving our plants a local source for water vapour, we can satisfy them without any discomfort to ourselves. If you have some container that has no spare room for peat or a similar substance, you can get a similar effect by putting pebbles or gravel at the bottom of the container and adding water so that it does not quite cover them. You then stand the pot on top. The water vapour will still rise round the plant, but the pebbles or gravel will stop the base of the pot coming into contact with the water. Plants that normally grow on dry land do not appreciate having their roots in water; they are not adapted for it and are liable to rot, so do keep the bottom of the pot clear of water. If you do have room for peat or vermiculite, you can make it look more attractive by collecting moss and placing it on top, but this is only done for appearance and does not make the filling any more effective.

DRAUGHTS

Another situation that is best avoided in the house is one that is in a draught. A perpetual draught will generally kill a plant and even a position where the opening of a door causes a draught is unsatisfactory, if the door is in frequent use. It is not entirely clear why this should be so, but presumably the combination of low temperature with drying conditions is inimicable to plant growth. In any case, whatever the cause, the practical applications are clear enough; do not put plants in draughty conditions. One should distinguish, perhaps, between draughty and airy conditions. Many plants relish abundant supplies of fresh air and some will not be very happy without such conditions. It is the localized current of cold air playing continuously on the plant that has the bad effect. The temporary effect of opening the door is less liable to be harmful and in normal conditions will be taken by the plant without bad results. It is only if the door is going to be used extremely frequently that the resultant draughts will cause damage. If you avoid putting your plants either in a draught or immediately above a fire, there are really no other places in the house where some plant cannot be found to grow suitably.

TYPES OF POT

We were talking earlier of plunging the plant-pot in some insulating material. You may well want to know which pots are the most satisfactory: the red clay pots, that have been in use for more than 100 years or the relatively modern plastic pots. This will not concern you when you buy your plant; you have to take the pot in which the nurseryman has planted it, but if you are successful and want eventually to move your plant into a larger pot, you may well be concerned. It is not a question to which it is easy to give an answer that is not hedged in by ifs and buts, except in certain cases. There seems no doubt at all that African violets (saintpaulias) do far better in plastic pots, and with certain other plants they also seem to have some advantages. Against that, there are plants which seem to do better in clay pots. The plastic pots, probably, are slightly to be preferred. They are lighter and do not break if you drop them, although when they age they are liable to split. They are not porous, as clay pots are, so that if you have overwatered, it takes far longer for the damage to be undone. Since they are not porous the roots are not attracted to the edge of the pot in the way that they are with clay pots, but tend to spread through the soil ball in a more regular manner. In a clay pot, the roots tend to go round the edges of the soil ball, nearest the wall of the pot, as this is the part of the pot where the soil is in its most satisfactory state. There is water vapour here being transmitted through the clay and also the soil is aerated well here. The centre of the soil ball is only colonized by the roots after they have already girdled the pot, whereas in the plastic pot the roots tend to behave in a manner more akin to what they would do in natural conditions; descending and then branching out, so that an adequate root system is developed somewhat more rapidly in the plastic pot.

Again, since the plastic pot is not porous, the soil will not need watering so frequently. Apart from the amount that the roots absorb, it is only lost through evaporation at the surface, not all the way round as in a clay pot. But if you have plunged the pot in peat or some other substance, this evaporation is considerably less, even in a clay pot, so this advantage is not so much to the benefit of the house-plant owner as to the benefit of the nurseryman. This greater retention of water has its dangers as well, of course. We have already seen that if the plant is overwatered it will take far longer to dry out, and an additional point is that soil mixtures for plastic pots must be somewhat more open and rapidly draining than mixtures for clay pots. Otherwise there is a risk of the soil becoming sour. You can guard against this by placing a handful of charcoal at the base of the pot, but it is an additional hazard. From the nurseryman's point of view the advantages of the plastic pot far outweight the disadvantages, so it is probable that house-plants will be sent out in plastic pots more and more frequently and that the clay pot will eventually disappear.

COMPOSTS

Assuming that you are successful in growing your house-plants, the time will come when your plant will have become too large for the pot in which it was growing when you bought it. You will have to move it on to a larger pot. At this stage the question of potting composts will come up. Now, if you read any gardening book written between 1760 and 1960 you will find that the recommended composts, although differing in detail, are mostly composed of loam, peat, leafmould and sand. The largest proportion of these composts was composed of the loam. Such mixtures are still to be preferred, but the amount of available loam is running out. Loam is a rather imprecise term and the writers of past days meant a fibrous, crumbly soil that was rich in humus. The usual way of obtaining this was to take up the top spit from pasture fields and stack it for a year, during which time it would rot down into an extremely fertile soil. People who live in the country can probably still go out and collect loam from the edges of woods and copses, but for the nurseryman, who wants enough, not not for just a few pots but for thousands, the supply is a major headache. As a result, people are turning more and more to the so-called soilless composts.

The main bulk of these is composed of peat. At the moment there is plenty of peat about so there should be little risk of supplies of this failing for some time. When it is dry, peat is light, which cuts down transport costs, and another advantage is that it is sterile, so that there is no risk of soil-borne diseases being introduced with it. When loam was used, it had to be sterilized with steam, an expensive process. This would kill off all weed seeds, fungus spores and most bacteria, so that the plant was not at risk. Soilless composts make this process unnecessary. The peat in the soilless composts is generally mixed with a certain amount of grit or sharp sand, which is also sterile and is used only to improve the physical quality of the compost. The grit helps to aerate it and to give good drainage. The resultant mixture is very satisfactory for the plant from the structural point of view. The roots will penetrate it easily and the compost will not become waterlogged.

Unfortunately, neither peat nor sand contain any plant nutrients. We know, more or less, what minerals are necessary for plant growth and it is comparatively easy for the agricultural scientist to calculate and prescribe a mixture which can be added to this inert compost and which will supply all the nutrients that the plant would normally obtain from the loam. However, the nutrients in the loam are released to the plant rather slowly over a long period, while those that are mixed in with the soilless compost tend to be washed out after about a year. For this initial year the plants appear to grow splendidly, but the technique is still not thoroughly developed and we do not really know what the long-term effects may be. The various plant foods that are on the market have been developed to assist plants growing in a loam compost, and it will now be necessary to obtain food mixtures that are especially compounded for these soilless composts. These will have to be applied regularly after the first year. If for any reason, you are unable to feed the plant regularly, symptoms of starvation—stunted growth, small, very dark green leaves, and so on—will show themselves much more rapidly than would be the case with a loam compost. Another minor disadvantage of these soilless composts is that if they dry out, you have to immerse the pot in a bucket of water and leave it there for sometime in order to get the compost thoroughly re-moistened.

Against these disadvantages, we have in soilless compost one that is physically ideal for plant growth and a balance of nutrients that is the best, so far as our present knowledge goes. This has resulted in many very fine plants being grown, and the plants appear to be perfectly healthy. Some plants seem to do better than others, begonias, for example, grow exceptionally well, but the majority of plants will thrive if adequately treated.

The loam compost was a more variable medium as the amount of difference in the chemical and physical composition of various loams is considerable. On the other hand, the loam contained a reserve of nutrients, which was only released very slowly to the plant. With this loam in the compost, it was very unlikely that the plant would show starvation symptoms if feeding was not regularly applied. Modern thinking at the moment is trying to combine the two processes, by making a basically soilless compost, but including a small proportion of loam as a standby. In a normal loam compost, such as the John Innes Potting Compost (J.I.P.)* the proportion of loam to peat and sand is over 50%; in the new mixtures it is probably only 10% or a little more. This has the advantage of conserving loam on the one hand and yet making the soilless mixture not entirely dependent on added nutrients for its power of providing plant food.

POTTING-ON

If you are successful in growing your house-plants, they will

* This is made in the proportion of 7 parts of loam to 3 parts of peat and 2 parts of sharp sand, all parts by bulk. To this is added $\frac{3}{4}$ ounce of ground chalk and either 4, 8, or 12 ounces of the John Innes Base fertilizer to each bushel. The amount of the J. I. Base depends on the size of the pot you are using; the larger the pot, the larger the amount of the base. The quantity of chalk added should be increased in the same proportions.

eventually grow too large for the pots in which they were growing when you bought them and you will have to 'pot them on'. We will discuss the actual technique of doing this shortly, but it will first be necessary for you to decide in what compost the plant was originally growing. If it is sent out from the nursery in a loam compost, then it is best either to buy some John Innes ready-mixed, or to mix some up for yourself. If it is in a soilless compost, then you must buy some of that. It would be risky to have a plant growing partly in a loam compost and partly in a soilless compost, as the two composts need different treatment, both for feeding and for watering. The large growers will probably state on their labels in what compost the plants are growing; with smaller firms you may have to inquire, although the appearance of the two composts is somewhat different and you may well be able to distinguish the two by inspection.

Repotting is not a very difficult operation. If you take your plant, turn it upside down and tap the edge of the pot against a hard surface such as a potting-bench, if you have one, or, if not, something like a draining-board, you will find that the contents of the pot can easily be extracted in one piece. You should put your fingers around the base of the stem of the plant, so that the whole plant does not fall out on to the floor. If the soil-ball appears to be absolutely full of roots, then the plant will need potting-on.

This operation should take place in late April or in May when the plant is starting to make its new growth. Do not attempt to do it later than mid-June. If the plant appears to require it after this, you must just feed it for the remainder of the summer and autumn. It will not need any feeding in the winter. The time to repot a plant is about four days after you last watered it. You do not want it to be too dry, otherwise the soil may fall from the roots when you take the plant from its old pot, and you do not want it too wet, as you have to water

1. *Aechmea rhodocyanea*

2. *Aphelandra
squarrosa
louisae*

3. Back: *Aralia elegantissima*; left: *Ficus pumila*; right: *Begonia masoniana*

4. *Araucaria excelsa*

5. *Asplenium nidus*

6. *Begonia rex*

7. *Beloperone guttata*

8. *Calathea insignis*

9. *Calathea louisae*

10. Left: *Chlorophytum comosum variegatum*; centre: *Cissus antarctica*; right: *Hedera helix* 'Little Diamond'

11. Left: *Codiaeum variegatum pictum*; centre: *Sansevieria trifasciata laurentii*; right: *Peperomia magnoliaefolia*

12. *Cryptanthus
tricolor*

13. Left: *Dracaena sanderiana*; foreground: *Peperomia hederaefolia*; right: *Asplenium nidus*

14. Left: X *Fatshedera lizei*;
centre: *Peperomia caperata*;
back: *Dracaena fragrans
massangeana*

15. *Ficus benjamina*

16. *Ficus elastica decora*

it when repotting is finished. The new mixture that you are going to add should also have been watered about four days before you are going to use it. It should look moist, but should not stick to your fingers. However, if it is rather on the dry side, no harm will come.

It is best with the smaller-sized pots to pot-on to one 2 inches more in diameter. Thus you pot from a 3-inch into a 5-inch pot and from a 5-inch into a 7-inch pot. Where the pot is larger than 7 inches, which means that the plant in it is a fairly large one, pot-on an inch at a time. Take the larger pot, put some crocks, concave-side downwards, or gravel in the bottom, if you are using a soil compost, and then put some of the new compost on to this. Specialist growers generally send out their plants without crocks at the base, as they are able to make a compost that drains very rapidly and does not get sodden. This has the advantage that more soil can be got into the pot. You are probably safe to do this with soil-less composts, but, unless you are sure of your potting compost, it is safer to crock the pots. Place the plant with its old soil-ball in the centre. The soil level should be about 1 inch below the rim of the pot, so that if you have not put enough new soil in, take out the old plant and add more. If you have put too much, take out the plant and remove some of the soil. Once the level is right, fill in all the intervening space between the old soil-ball and the pot wall with the new mixture, pressing it down well with your thumbs. Smooth the soil so that the surface is level, give a good watering, by filling the pot with water to the brim, and the task is finished. If you are using old pots, clean the inside with a handful of newspaper. New clay pots should be soaked for 24 hours before being used; new plastic pots need no preparation.

Once the plant is potted-on, you will find that the soil will not dry out so rapidly as it did in the old pot and you will have to water less frequently while the plant sends roots into the new soil. In the same way you will not need to feed the plant for the season.

WATERING

We have touched lightly on the questions of watering (see pp. 15, 18 and 22) and feeding (see p. 16), but these are the real touchstones of successful house-plant cultivation and we must now consider them further. Most losses among house-plants are caused by the plants being drowned with kindness. If they are given too much water, they will rot and die. We saw in the first chapter that plants do not grow at the same rate all the year round. When a plant is growing, making new stems and leaves above ground and throwing new roots out underground, it will require a good deal of water. But even so the matter is not clear cut. A period of dull and cool conditions will temporarily slow growth down while, if it turns very warm and bright, growth will be accelerated. During the winter, when there is comparatively little light, growth is very slow, even though the temperatures may be quite high (there are exceptions to this, but not so far as house-plants are concerned), so the plant requires less water.

The water is lost in two ways: some will just evaporate from the surface of the soil, so the warmer the room the more rapidly the water will evaporate. The rest is taken up by the roots, so that the more active the roots the more water is used. Here again there are exceptions. Some tropical plants are epiphytes; they do not grow on or in the ground, but perch on rocks or tree boughs. They have roots, but they are only used as an anchorage and do not take up nourishment as most roots do. Some of these are cultivated as house-plants. The most important of these are the bromeliads (aechmea, cryptanthus, neoregelia, vriesia) and, as you will see in the next chapter, they need special treatment. The peperomias are partly epiphytic; they have a very small root system and obtain

34

most of their nourishment from the atmosphere. These are the only exceptions that we need bother about. Otherwise it may be stated fairly dogmatically that the amount of water a plant requires depends on its immediate conditions. At one time it will need a lot, at another time very little.

A safe rule of thumb is to inspect your plants daily and when the surface of the soil looks dry, water the next day. That is because the surface always dries out first and the soil is probably still moist underneath. When you do water, fill the pot to the brim, so that the water will permeate all the soil in the pot. Sometimes at the end of winter, when the soil has been kept fairly dry, you may find that when you water, the soil has shrunk and the water appears to run straight through the pot. If this happens, put the pot into a bucket of water, with the water level above that of the pot, and leave it until bubbles stop rising from the surface of the compost. Then take it out and firm the soil all round the wall of the pot with your thumbs. Rain water is the best to use, if you have the facilities for collecting it, and it should, ideally, be at room temperature. If you are using tap water, mix a little hot water in with it. It will do no harm if it is slightly tepid, but very cold water may slow the plant down. If possible always have your water at the same temperature. This is a counsel of perfection and many people grow plants perfectly happily without all this fuss, but results are better if a little care is taken. Indeed, in the case of the African violet, it is one of the main contributions to success. Most other plants are far less demanding.

FEEDING

Feeding is rarely necessary the year that you buy your house-plant or the year after repotting. The only time that it does any good is when the plant is in active and visible growth, which means to all intents and purposes between May and August, but it is no use if the plant has only a few roots. Feeds come in various forms. The most popular are in liquid form and are added to the water in the watering-can. But there are also powders that you sprinkle over the soil surface, and even pills that you insert in the soil. All these will come with directions and these should be carefully followed. With the liquid feeds an application once every three weeks is sufficient and a similar interval is usually recommended for the solid feeds. Plants cannot be hurried. You may think that your plant looks a little starved and be tempted to feed it every week. This does no good at all. The plant can only take up so much food and any excess will just be wasted and could even do the plant harm. The same would apply to doubling the amount of feed at any one time. Small amounts at regular intervals will keep your plants in the best condition.

CLEANING

Hygiene does not usually present many difficulties. We saw in the first chapter (p. 12) that it was bad for the leaves to become covered with dust and they should be cleaned at fairly frequent intervals. Once a week is the best, but, if time does not allow, a longer interval will not do much harm. Cleaning is best done with cotton wool dipped in tepid water, and equal attention should be paid to the underside of the leaf, even though you may not see it. Young leaves that have just unfurled are very delicate and should not be touched until they have become fairly rigid and will not tear. Milk or flat beer will give an enhanced glossiness to the leaves, but may clog the pores. With plants that have a very large number of small leaves, such as some of the peperomias, it may be easier to clean the leaves by holding the plant under a gently-running tap in such a way that the leaves are moistened, without the soil being touched at all. This means that the plant is either held sideways or upside down. The leaves can also be cleaned in a bowl of tepid water in this way. Syringing the leaves with a fine spray, such as a scent spray, is beneficial to the plant in giving a moist atmosphere, but is not much use for removing dust. A spray that is sufficiently strong to do this is liable to damage the furniture and carpets, so that if you wish to clear your dust with a strongish spray, you will have to remove your plants to some place, such as the draining-board, where a little surplus water will do no harm. Once this is done, they can be replaced. During the summer, plants can be stood outside in gentle rain, which will not only clean the dust, but will benefit them in other ways, but this can only be done when the weather is warm, so far as the majority of house-plants is concerned. Otherwise the chill would undo the good that the rain had performed.

PESTS

As a general rule, pests are not much trouble with house-plants, but there is one exception. This is the red spider mite. The mite is not a spider and is not always red. It is a very minute creature which congregates on the underside of the leaves and sucks the nourishment from them. Leaves become discoloured and get a characteristic rough feel, when you handle them. The pest usually occurs only when the atmosphere is very dry and so, if you can keep the atmosphere round the plants moist in the way we have suggested above, and if you can find the time to syringe the plants fairly frequently in hot weather, it is very unlikely that you will be troubled with this. If, however, it does occur, there are two methods of treatment. The most effective is to apply systemic insecticides. These are given either in the watering-can or syringed on to the leaves. They are taken up by the plant and poison any insect that sucks the sap. Unfortunately, the most effective of these are really deadly poisons, which need to be handled with great care and to be kept very carefully away, not only from children, but from everybody else. Keep them, indeed, under lock and

37

key. A far safer method is a white oil emulsion. This is bought easily enough from horticultural sundriesmen and is diluted with water. It is probably best that this is done in a bucket, and the leaves of the plant are then immersed in this bucket, in such a way that all the leaves are covered with the liquid on both surfaces. This is essential as the emulsion works by contact with the mites, and any that escape contact will continue breeding at the usual fantastic rate. Plants with very large leaves, such as the rubber tree or *Monstera pertusa*, can have every individual leaf treated, as they will probably be too large to immerse in a bucket. Again you do not want the emulsion to soak into the soil, so the plant is turned upside down and only the leaves put into the bucket. The treatment needs to be repeated after a week.

Another pest which occasionally attacks large-leaved plants, mainly rubber plants and crotons, is the scale insect. These congregate on the underside of the leaves and also on the stems. They are greyish in colour, oval-shaped, about 1 inch long and never seem to move. They are only a nuisance if their presence has been overlooked. If you inspect the underside of the leaves of your rubber plants or crotons about once a month, you will be able to see if there are any of these little pests. They are easily recognizable and are usually removed with a matchstick, on the end of which a little cotton-wool has been fixed, so that the leaf is not damaged. Sometimes the cotton-wool is dipped in methylated spirit, which helps to kill the scale insects.

Greenfly will turn up from time to time, but is easily controlled nowadays, as the makers of insecticides make an aerosol pack to deal with this pest, as well as with thrips, which you are unlikely to see in any case. Control by this means is very easy, but it is important to follow the maker's directions exactly. Use the aerosol sparingly as the insecticide is very concentrated in this form, and take particular care if using it on flowers or young shoots and leaves.

DISEASES

Fungus diseases are even less liable to occur, but sometimes either a dry atmosphere or a rather cold spell may result in the appearance of begonia mildew. This is a whitish mould which appears on the leaves of begonias. It is not at all easy to treat satisfactorily and the best thing to do is to remove all affected leaves and hope that the newly-emerging ones will be clean. In the nursery they are fumigated with colloidal sulphur and steam, but this is not possible in the home. It is not very frequently met with and one must just hope for the best.

FROST

If plants are placed against the window, they should be brought into the room when severe weather is forecast, otherwise there is a risk of the leaves becoming frosted, even though the room temperature may be more than adequate. Presumably this would not be necessary with double-glazing, but with a single pane, it is by no means unusual to see ice on the inside of the glass, even with a radiator directly underneath the window. If you are taken unawares and a plant does become frosted, the best hope of recovery is to insure that it thaws out very slowly. Remove the plant, therefore, to your coldest room and syringe the leaves with cold water. After 24 hours it can be brought back to its required temperature. You must keep it on the dry side until it shows signs of recovery by making some growth and you should continue to be sparing with water for some time.

CULTIVATION TROUBLES

Occasionally as one looks at one's plants, one finds various sorts of unsatisfactory behaviour, for which it is not always easy to give a clear-cut remedy. Sometimes the matter is simple. Variegated plants will sometimes throw a shoot that is unvariegated. If this happens, chop the offending part of the plant off.

However, do not be too hasty; some plants such as the variegated *Hoya carnosa*, and the ivy known as 'Golden Jubilee' do not develop their variegation until the leaves are fully developed. The worst offenders are the tradescantias and they develop their variegation early.

Although most house-plants are not grown for their flowers, with those that are, it is irritating when the flower buds drop off as they are getting close to flowering. This may be due to a large number of causes and it is not always easy to find out what the actual reason is. The main causes for this tiresome habit are the plant being too wet or too dry. Other possibilities include insufficient light, and the fact that the plant has been placed in a draughty position. The most likely ones are those due to the condition of the soil. One is so liable (quite rightly) to fear overwatering, that one may let the plant become too dry. Plants will generally take more water than usual when producing buds and flowers. However, excessively damp soil will also cause bud drop.

You will always get a few of the lower leaves yellowing and dropping off in most plants, but this should not happen with *Ficus elastica*, or any plant with fairly leathery leaves. Excessive yellowing and leaf drop is almost always due to excess water; the other main reason would be too low temperatures. Sometimes the leaves develop unsightly brown spots. These are once again usually due to water, although it may be that it is water resting on the leaves that is causing these spots, rather than too much in the soil. Occasionally the edges of the leaves turn brown. There is not much that can be done about this, which usually only happens in the winter, except trimming the unsightly portions off with nail scissors. It is only a few plants that develop this tiresome habit. The old variegated *Fatsia japonica* was a particularly bad offender, but the more recent strain seems to have developed some immunity and rarely browns at the edges.

40

Very occasionally you may have a plant that makes no growth, or very little. In this case it is as well first to check that the plant is getting sufficient warmth. We have seen that some plants will not make any growth if the temperature falls too low, even though the plant is not damaged, and this would be a cause for your plant making poor growth. If the temperature seems to be correct, the soil mixture may be wrong. This is unlikely to happen with plants purchased from well-known growers, but is always possible with plants that have been grown by amateurs, so if the plant you acquired at the Bring-and-Buy sale is not doing too well, you might well try repotting it. We do not want to slander all amateurs, any more than we would extol all nurserymen, but a nurseryman who puts his plants in the wrong soil mixtures would not stay in business long, so they tend to be more reliable, not from any excess of virtue, but for purely business reasons. No house-plant makes a great deal of growth in any one year in any case, so if some growth is being made, rest content.

CLOSED CONTAINERS

Of late years many people have been putting their house-plants into closed containers. From the point of view of growing plants, the best is a sort of miniature greenhouse. This is a glass-framed box, like a tropical fish tank, with an electric heating-unit, which is thermostatically controlled and over-head, built-in illumination. This enables one to grow plants that require higher temperatures than those that you can normally provide and, indeed, to grow plants that would not normally be considered house-plants at all. They are quite expensive to purchase and to run, but they do enlarge the range of possible plants to grow.

BOTTLE GARDENS

Bottle gardens are also popular. In this case, the bottom of a large bottle or carboy is filled with a moderately rich potting compost about 6–9 inches deep, and some charcoal is usually added to help keep it sweet. It is poured in through a paper funnel, so that the sides do not become covered with soil. Once you have put in your plants, it is often a good idea to direct a little additional soil around the holes that you have excavated, so that the surface is entirely level. Plants are inserted by means of a trowel or two spoons, both fixed to the end of a long stick. You should select plants that do not grow too quickly and plant them working in towards the centre of the bottle from the sides. The soil is watered by allowing the liquid to trickle gently down the sides of the bottle and it is as well to practise doing this before you put in the soil and plants. If you cork the bottle firmly, once it has been planted, the plants will grow successfully, but the glass will be coated with steam and it will not be easy to see the plants. On the other hand you will probably not need to water the plants ever again. If you allow a little ventilation, the water vapour will escape and the glass will be clear, but you will need to water from time to time, although far less frequently than you would if the plants were in individual pots. Even with the slowest growing plants, there is liable to come a time when the plants become too large for their bottle, but it is not possible to remove them and when this happens, the only practical thing is to find another bottle and begin again. When we come to describe plants in detail, we will mention those that are most suitable for bottle gardens. It is an operation of some delicacy to make a good bottle garden, and those who are like one of the authors and somewhat ham-handed, should not attempt it. Some people place an electric lamp above their bottle gardens, which gives an agreeable effect and supplies the plants with additional illumination.

CHAPTER III

WHAT HOUSE-PLANTS TO GROW

This chapter will describe all the most popular house-plants that are being grown at the moment. Every so often you will find new plants being introduced, but it is best for the amateur to wait a short while to see how they work out in practice. There are very many attractive plants that we can grow comparatively easily in the greenhouse, but which are very difficult to grow in our rooms. This is mainly due to the dry atmospheres that we like to live in. Even with the methods suggested in the last chapter for giving a moist atmosphere around the plants, the result may yet be too dry for some. Illumination may also have its effects. The brightest position in a room will appear comparatively shady to the plant, and those that require a lot of light to function successfully will find the house too dark. Even plants placed in windows will only be illuminated from one side. This may be obviated in houses with bay windows, but even there the light only comes from the sides and there is none descending from above. We have, therefore, to restrict ourselves to those plants that will grow successfully in room conditions.

In order to be a good house-plant, the plant should be attractive to look at in all seasons of the year, which means that it should be evergreen, and that the leaves should be worth looking at. Some plants will produce their flowers over a long period, but most have a comparatively short flowering season

43

and the plant may not be very attractive for the rest of the year. On the other hand, many plants will have attractive leaves, but the flowers may be inconspicuous. It is quite a rarity to find plants that combine these attractions, although there will be one or two in our list.

Some of the plants can be easily propagated in the home from cuttings, while others need greenhouse conditions and more heat than most of us can provide. Where home propagation is easy, we will describe it and if no methods are mentioned, it may be concluded that propagation is difficult, or even that it cannot be done through cuttings at all. *Philodendron bipinnatifidum*, for example, must be raised from seed.

As far as house-plants are concerned you will be dealing either with stem cuttings or with leaf cuttings. Stem cuttings are usually taken when the stem is fairly firm; soft young growth is liable to rot off. They are usually about 3 inches long and are trimmed to a leaf joint. The lower leaves are removed and the cutting is put in a mixture such as half peat and half sharp sand, or vermiculite. When the cuttings are inserted, they should be watered in and placed in a warm position. It is quite a practical idea to put the pot containing cuttings in a polythene bag, which should not be allowed to touch the cuttings. This prevents the cuttings from drying out. Once the cuttings are rooted they should be put in a more nutritive mixture as neither of the rooting media mentioned have any nutriment.

As far as leaf cuttings are concerned, the leaf and a portion of the stalk is removed and inserted in the rooting media. Otherwise the practice does not differ. Rex begonias need a slightly different treatment which is mentioned on page 57.

A NOTE ON LATIN NAMES

If you are going to grow house-plants, there is no way of avoiding those jaw-breaking Latin names. They look very formidable at first, but in a short time you can get used to them. Most of them have some reason for their existence and it may make them a little less formidable if we consider what these reasons are.

Every plant has two Latin names. The first name, which is spelt with a capital, is the generic name. A genus of plants is considered to have a number of features in common, which are not found in the same combination in any other genus. All botanical names are a matter of convenience; they are given so that other botanists or gardeners know what plant you are talking about. Using vernacular common names may sometimes lead to confusion. There are three or four different plants known as Bachelors' Buttons; Reed Grass is a name that covers at least two kinds of grass; Hemlock is a tree in North America and a herbaceous plant in this country. When using Latin names, we at least know to which Hemlock or to which Bachelors' Buttons the other speaker is referring.

The names that are chosen for the genus may either describe the plant in some way or may be chosen to honour some botanist of the past. Thus, in the plants we are discussing, *Begonia* is named after a M. Michel Begon, who encouraged botanists, although he himself was Governor of Canada at the time that the country was a French possession. *Dieffenbachia* commemorates a famous Austrian gardener, Herr Dieffenbach. *Neoregelia* is named after a famous Russian botanist, Regel. *Sansevieria* commemorates, rather oddly, Raimond de Sansgrio, who was Prince of Sanseviero. *Saintpaulia* is named after the botanist who first discovered the plant, Baron Walter von Saint Paul-Illaire. *Schefflera* is named after a botanist from Danzig, J. G. Scheffler, while *Tradescantia* is named after Charles I's gardener, the famous John Tradescant.

If the generic name is to be descriptive of the plant it is liable to be derived not from Latin but from Greek. Thus the very first name in the plants discussed is *Aechmea rhodocyanea*.

Aechmea comes from a Greek word meaning a spine; the calyx of each flower is somewhat spiny, while *rhodocyanea* comes from the Greek word for rose, *rhodos*, and the Greek word for blue, *cyaneos*, and describes the pink inflorescence (the group of flowers) and the blue flowers. You can find the word *rhodos* again in rhododendron; the word *dendron* is the Greek for tree, so rhododendron means the pink tree. In the same way *Philodendron* means a plant that is fond of trees; a perfectly sensible name when we realize that most philodendrons grow up trees in the wild. Some of these Greek-derived names are still somewhat obscure, even when we find out what the Greek words mean. *Aphelandra*, for example, comes from two words meaning simple and male. The male part of the plant is the anther and in *Aphelandra* the anthers have only a single cell. *Aglaonema* comes from two words meaning 'shining thread', though why this should be regarded as applicable to aglaonemas is anyone's guess.

Sometimes the names are derived from the local vernacular names. *Codiaeum* is a latinization of the Javanese *kodiho*; *Fatsia* comes from the Japanese *Fa-tsi*. So you can see that the names are not meaningless, even though it may sometimes be difficult to find out what the meaning is.

The second name is the specific name. This generally either describes the plant or commemorates its discoverer (or possibly some friend of the discoverer's). Thus *Calathea insignis* suggests that this is a striking or remarkable plant; *insignis* is the Latin for remarkable, but *Calathea louisae* means that this plant commemorates a Louise, in this case the wife of the king of the Belgians, Queen Louise. In the same way *Begonia masoniana* is named in honour of Mr. Maurice Mason, who first introduced the plant to this country, and *Impatiens petersiana* honours a Mr. Peters.

The descriptive names are usually quite helpful, if you understand Latin. For example *scandens* means climbing, so we know that *Philodendron scandens* must be a climbing plant. *Hederaefolia* means that the plant has leaves like a *Hedera*, an ivy, so *Peperomia hederaefolia* means that this peperomia has leaves like an ivy (which it has not, but that is the botanists' fault, not ours).

Sometimes you will find a third or varietal name. This is generally descriptive. Plants with variegated leaves are usually given the varietal name *variegatus*. *Ficus elastica decora* means that this is the handsome variety of *F. elastica*. Occasionally the varietal name is also commemorative. Thus *Monstera pertusa borsigiana* means that this particular form of the perforated (*pertusa*) monstera was distributed from Borsig's nursery, and *Sansevieria trifasciata laurentii* commemorates a M. Laurent.

You can see, we hope, that these difficult names are not really just a concatenation of meaningless syllables. They do have a meaning and very often there is no English name to use in their place. After a very short time they become quite natural and you will use them in preference to the English names. It is easier to say *Tradescantia* Rochford's Quicksilver rather than Rochford's Quicksilver Wandering Jew.

Sometimes plants have a third name and you may be rather puzzled by seeing that sometimes this third name is, like the other two names, in Latin and sometimes in English. Provided that this is done consistently (which is not, alas, always the case) there is a reason for this, which is satisfactory for the botanist, although for the simple plant-lover it may appear finicky.

Among wild plants you may frequently find some which differ in some way from the majority of their fellows. The most common variation is when a plant that normally has coloured flowers bears white flowers. White heather and white bluebells are not typical, but are found quite often. When a variation from the norm occurs in the wild state, particularly when it

47

occurs fairly frequently, botanists give it a third or varietal name, which is usually prefixed by var., an abbreviation of the Latin *varietas*. Thus Scottish heather is *Calluna vulgaris*, but the white heather is *C. vulgaris* var. *alba* (*alba* is the Latin for white). If the varietal name is in Latin you are justified in assuming that the variation occurs in nature and more or less frequently. It is also probable that, if the variety is self-fertilized, the resultant seedlings will have the same varied characteristics as the parent.

In the course of cultivation other varieties may arise that have not been found among wild plants. Very often only a part of the plant will show this variation. One branch may have variegated leaves, or one part of the plant may bear flowers of a different colour from the rest. These are known as 'sports', and the sporting portion of the plant can be propagated by cuttings, or by some other vegetative means. Provided that the stock remains healthy one can continue propagating indefinitely, and eventually a small twig can become the progenitor of thousands of plants. Normally these will not come true from seed. These varieties that occur only in cultivation are termed 'cultivars' and are given names not in Latin, but in the vernacular of the country in which they occur. As a general rule (but there are many exceptions, particularly among annual plants) cultivars will not come true from seed, but can only be propagated by vegetative means: cuttings or layers. Plants that have been propagated in this way are known as clones. We can best illustrate this perhaps by considering some of the ivies, *Hedera helix*. You will observe considerable variation in the leaf-shapes of wild ivies and one of the more attractive is when the central lobe is so elongated that the leaf looks like an arrow-head. This is *Hedera helix* var. *sagittifolia*, and it is not so very uncommon in the wild. Now, suppose you are a nurseryman and have a house full of variegated ivies. You notice one that has produced a branch with much smaller leaves than the rest of the plant. You take this branch and propagate it until you have enough plants to market this new variety. We say 'variety', but that would not be correct botanically; it is really a cultivar, so we must give it an English name. Such a plant is *H. helix* 'Little Diamond'. It is a typographic convention to put cultivar names in single quotes. Unfortunately many of the earlier nurserymen would latinize their cultivar names, so that we have *Ficus elastica schryveriana*, which should, correctly, be written *Ficus elastica* 'Schryveriana', and, even so, 'Schryveriana' is not really acceptable as a cultivar name. Doubtless eventually all will be straightened out, but the matter is rather confused at the present time.

CLASSIFYING HOUSE-PLANTS

House-plants can conveniently be divided into three groups according to the winter temperatures required. Those that require a minimum of 45°F are described as needing cool conditions and a 'C' will be placed after their name in the list. Those that require warm conditions with a minimum of 65°F will have a 'W', while those that require conditions intermediate between the two, a temperature of 55°F, will be designated 'I'. These temperatures are the average that should be maintained and occasional periods at 5° less will do no harm, though they should not occur if the soil is wet. When the plant is fairly dry it will tolerate temperatures considerably lower than those that are desirable, but it will not like them and may even be checked. However, a temporary breakdown in your heating arrangements should not do much harm even to 'W' plants, provided that they are not actually frosted. The roots will be affected, though, and water should only be given very sparingly for the next ten days, if such a disaster has occurred.

Aechmea rhodocyanea (I)

This belongs to the bromeliad family, of which the pineapple is probably the best known member. Many of its members, like this plant, grow in rain forests, perched on the boughs of the trees, not growing in the soil as most plants do. This means that the roots serve almost entirely for anchorage and do not take up nourishment in the way that terrestrial plants do. Thus, once you have bought a plant, you do not have to worry about repotting it. The plants have their leaves arranged in a rosette with an open centre that is generally referred to as the 'vase'. You should keep this vase filled with water, and if you can manage to obtain it rain water is definitely an advantage. There is no need to water the soil-ball, although it is a good idea to do this in very hot weather in the summer. The leaves are rather thick and leathery and are strap-shaped; they are grey-green in colour with horizontal light grey bands. The rosette in a large, mature plant may be as much as 2 feet across and 1 foot high.

The plant is usually offered for sale when the flower-stem is emerging. This is very spectacular, being covered with brilliant pink bracts, which also surround the flower head. The stem will eventually reach a height of 18 inches and from the thick cluster of pink bracts, small lavender-blue flowers emerge. These only last for a short time, but there are a very large number of them, so that flowering continues over several weeks and the bracts keep their colour for as long as six months.

Once flowering is over the main rosette will die, but there will probably be some small side-shoots around the base. These can be grown on. As the main rosette dies, it should be cut out with a sharp knife, taking care not to damage the rhizome to which the side-shoots will be attached. The plant should be put in a very well-lit position and during the winter the water placed in the vase should be slightly warm. During the summer very

50

minute doses of fertilizer (a liquid one is best for this purpose) can be added to the water in the vase at three-weekly intervals, but only very small doses should be given. Although Intermediate conditions are to be desired, it has caused a lot of surprise to find out what low temperatures many bromeliads will tolerate without ill effect. Gas fumes do not seem to upset these plants.

Aglaonema treubii (W)

There are quite a large number of aglaonemas grown, though they all look rather alike. They make compact little plants, developing a sort of trunk as they age. *Aglaonema treubii* has lance-shaped leaves, which may be 5 inches long, but are only 1½ inches across. They are a darkish green in colour, with irregular grey-green zones along the lateral veins. The plant belongs to the arum family and mature plants may produce small, white arum-like flowers that are followed by dark red berries. However, this is not likely to happen in the home. The plant does not require to be very well-lit, but will not be happy in too dark a position. Gas fumes it will not tolerate. Keep the atmosphere round it as moist as you can, but keep the compost on the dry side during the winter. Provided that you can give the high winter temperature required, this is an easy and attractive plant.

Aphelandra squarrosa louisae (Zebra Plant) (I)

This has an upright stem, which may eventually reach a height of 18 inches, and from which, at very short intervals, spring pairs of deep green, shiny leaves that are oblong-oval in shape. They may reach a length of 9 inches and a width of 4½ inches. All the principal veins of the leaf are picked out in ivory. When the plant becomes pot-bound it will produce pyramidal flower heads, which are composed of long green bracts from which the yellow flowers emerge. This used to happen quite

51

frequently with the first plants grown, but they have now largely been superseded by the varieties 'Brockfeld' and 'Silver Beauty', which have far more attractive leaves than the original introduction, but flower very little. 'Silver Beauty' indeed has considerably more ivory than green in the leaf and these leaves are set even closer together. 'Brockfeld' has a more pronounced ivory zone along the veins and larger leaves.

The plants are very greedy and need feeding during the growing season from mid-May to mid-August, and should really be repotted yearly. They should never be allowed to dry out and will need ample water during the summer otherwise their leaves droop quickly and spectacularly. When side-shoots appear they can be used as cuttings, but they will need a temperature of at least 65°F to root. No further attention should be required until the cuttings are rooted, which should be in three to five weeks. A very gentle pull will tell you if the cuttings are rooted. If there is any resistance, they probably are, and they should then be potted in some compost, as the peat and sand mixture has no nourishment. The plant will tolerate gas fumes, but it does not like them. A reasonable amount of light is required.

Aralia elegantissima (Spider Plant) (I, W)

Something seems to have happened to this plant. At one time it was thought to be one of the most difficult of all house-plants and only to be tried by experts. However, a quantity of seed has been imported and the resultant plants have proved themselves to be very accommodating. Although they prefer a moist atmosphere, they now seem to tolerate the dry atmosphere of rooms far better than the old plants did.

The plant is a slender shrub with narrow spidery leaves; each leaf is composed of from seven to ten leaflets that may be 3 inches long but are barely $\frac{1}{2}$ an inch across. These are a delightful coppery-red when young, but they become nearly black as they mature. As house-plants aralias will be from 6 inches to 2 feet high, but they can be grown on in greenhouses into quite large shrubs, when they lose their spidery leaves and produce, instead, much wider leaves like those of a horse chestnut, which are less attractive than the juvenile leaves that we see in the house-plant form.

The plant needs a fairly well-lit position, but should be shielded from strong sunlight in the summer. Like most house-plants it is kept as dry as possible during the winter, although the soil should not become dust dry. It is very prone to attacks from red spider mites, so that it is useful to spray the foliage at regular intervals, sparingly in the winter, but frequently in spring and summer, and you should try to maintain a moist atmosphere just around the plant. It will tolerate gas fumes in moderation, but would not be happy in a room that is constantly heated by an open gas fire.

No plant called aralia probably has any right to that name. The correct name for our plant is *Dizygotheca elegantissima*, which is rather an ugly name, while the correct name of *Aralia sieboldii*, which you may sometimes see offered, is the much nicer *Fatsia japonica*, which you will find later on in this list.

Araucaria excelsa (Norfolk Island Pine) (C)

Probably the most well-known araucaria is the monkey puzzle tree, but the present plant is far more elegant. In the wild it makes a very large tree, plants up to 200 feet high have been recorded, but it also makes a very elegant small tree for pot work. The branches, which radiate horizontally to give a pyramid-shaped plant, are covered with soft, light green, needle-like leaves for the whole of their length, so that the plant is very densely leafy. The house-plant forms are compact varieties that grow slowly and do not need much repotting.

The plants should be given a very well-lit position and should be turned around at intervals, so that the growths remain symmetrical; if the plant is left in the same position, the shoots will all tend to grow towards the light and the attractive symmetry will be lost. Cool conditions are perfectly satisfactory for this plant, which has been grown out of doors in Cornwall, though it does not always survive there for long. As it is only potted-on at long intervals it is probable that soilless composts would not prove very satisfactory for the Norfolk Island pine. It is tolerant of gas and oil fumes.

Asplenium nidus (Bird's-nest Fern) (I, W)

This splendid fern is usually bought as quite a small plant, but if given the correct warm, moist conditions, can eventually grow into a very large plant. Specimens are known that have fronds as long as 4 feet and 8 inches across, although you are not likely to get plants of these dimensions in your home. The fronds are undivided, not unlike the hart's-tongue fern of our hedgerows, but far larger and of a darker green. To do best it needs warm winter conditions, but it will survive under Intermediate temperatures. It is practically an epiphyte and will grow extremely well in soilless composts. It is absolutely vital that the compost should be very well drained as otherwise the plant may collapse. It is also necessary to maintain a moist atmosphere around the leaves, and this is best done by sinking the pot in a larger container containing peat, vermiculite or sphagnum moss, and keeping this moist. This will encourage the fern to produce aerial roots, which seem to contribute more nourishment than do the terrestrial ones.

The plant is tolerant of gas and oil fumes and requires a shady situation, although this should not be too dark. Plants with a black midrib will tolerate lower temperatures than those with a greenish midrib. Owing to its small amount of roots it cannot be fed in the normal way, but if minute amounts of fertilizer are dissolved in water, this can be sprayed on to the leaves. It is best, however, to buy a proper foliar feed as otherwise it is all too easy to damage the fronds by adding too much fertilizer to the water. They will do quite well without any feeding if conditions are right. This fern is not, in any case, the easiest of house-plants and should be treated with respect. Young plants grow well in bottle gardens.

Begonia (I)

There are a very large number of begonias that can be grown as house-plants, but we are only going to deal with two sorts here.

Begonia masoniana (Iron Cross Begonia)

All the begonias we shall be talking about have leaves that form a roughly asymmetric triangle, although what should be the base of the triangle tends to be heart-shaped, and the other edges are more or less jagged. As regards the iron cross begonia, this jagged edge is not very marked. The leaves are about 5 inches long and 3 inches across and are green with a touch of grey over their main portion. The surface of the leaf is puckered, to give a somewhat mossy effect. Starting from the base of the leaf, and persisting for about half-way along the principal veins, are narrow purple zones that can be likened to the well-known German medal, as they are shaped in a similar manner.

All begonias have very fine roots and require a very light soil mixture—soilless composts suit them well. Otherwise they seem to do best in equal mixtures of leafmould, peat and sharp sand, with only a small proportion of loam. They will not tolerate oil or gas fumes, even in small quantities. Their presence will not kill the plants, but will cause them to drop their leaves and look unsightly. They require rather shady conditions, but if the situation is too dark the leaf colours will not develop properly. This plant has only been known since 1952, when that great collector of greenhouse plants, Mr. L.

Maurice Mason (after whom it is named) brought it to England from Singapore; its native habitat is not known.

Rex Begonias

Although there is a perfectly good species called *Begonia rex*, the Rex begonias are the result of hybridizing this with other species, the most important of which are *B. decora*, which brings red into the leaves, and *B. diadema*, which gives a very jagged leaf shape. The result of all this hybridizing has been a race of plants with extremely brilliantly coloured leaves, ranging from dark green with silver mottling to brilliant crimson, with almost every conceivable variation in between.

Rex begonias are not difficult to grow, although excessive dryness should be guarded against, as much as excessive wet. They do not like violent fluctuations of temperature and too much of this may result in the appearance of begonia mildew, the control of which entails cutting off all affected leaves and will certainly disfigure the plant. This is not a common complaint with this particular begonia and most growers are not troubled with it. Although we have marked these plants Intermediate, they will overwinter successfully under Cool conditions, although some leaves may be lost under these circumstances. However, fresh leaves will be formed in the summer and the fact that you cannot provide ideal winter temperatures need not prevent you growing these plants. They have even been known to regenerate after being frosted. They do best in a shady situation, but the shade should not be too heavy. Apparently in nature they grow in woodland that gives a dappled shade.

Both these and *B. masoniana* have a creeping rhizome (underground stem) and when this gets too long the plant should be taken from its pot and most of the old rhizome, which is no longer bearing leaves, should be cut away and the plant repotted in the same size pot as the one from which it was

56

taken. If you have a small greenhouse the plants can be easily propagated by means of leaf cuttings. A leaf is cut off and cut into squares about the size of postage stamps. These are laid on a mixture of peat and sand in a seed-box and kept moist but not sodden, in a temperature of 65°F. Tiny plants will arise from the base of the cut principal veins and these are grown on in as Warm conditions as you can provide. You could probably root them in the house, but they would not be easy to grow on.

Flowers are occasionally produced, but they are a rather dirty white and not particularly attractive. Their presence is generally a sign that the plant has become pot-bound. If you have a greenhouse, you might obtain some seed and be able to produce fresh begonias, among which there might be something particularly good. However, such hybrids turn up at rare intervals and it is more likely that you will get a lot of indifferent plants.

Beloperone guttata (Shrimp Plant) (C, I)

This is a comparatively recent introduction. It was first cultivated in 1936. The plant makes a small shrub, capable of reaching a height of 2 or 3 feet, but it is usually kept pruned and seldom exceeds $1\frac{1}{2}$ feet in height. It is one of the few house-plants that are grown for their flowers rather than for their leaves. Indeed, these are not remarkable, being oval in shape, rather small and of a soft green colour. If it comes to that, the flowers themselves are rather small and inconspicuous, but they emerge from a head of ruddy brown bracts that is shaped like the body of a shrimp. These flowers are produced almost continuously throughout the summer and autumn. In the early spring it is advisable to prune the branches back, so as to discourage the plant from becoming leggy and ungainly. It grows perfectly happily under Cool conditions, but the flowering season may be prolonged if warmer conditions are available, and if a little additional warmth can be given in spring, after the pruning, the plant will come sooner into blossom again.

The plants should be given the best-lit position available and do well if placed in windows. As we said in the last chapter, they should be removed from this position when severe frosts are expected. They seem to give little trouble and appreciate feeding during the summer.

Calathea (W)

There are a number of calatheas, all making rather small, compact plants with leaves of quite extraordinary loveliness. They all require similar treatment. This includes a warm, moist atmosphere and a shady situation. We have given them a 'W', but they seem to do quite well under Intermediate conditions. Sunlight falling on to the leaves causes them to curl up and sometimes they will then remain in this condition for two days or more. Although they require moist conditions they do not require much water around their roots, except at the height of their growing season, from June to August, and they like a very open compost. One would expect the soilless composts to be excellent for them. The underside of the leaf is often nearly as attractive as the upper side and they should be placed so that both surfaces can be appreciated. If plants get very large and tufty, they can be divided, but otherwise propagation is too difficult for amateurs. In order to grow really luxuriantly they need Warm conditions and so they will not be very active in cold seasons, unless you keep your house very warm in the summer, regardless of the outside temperatures. They are all suitable for bottle gardens.

Calathea insignis

Superlatively grown specimens of this plant are said to have leaves up to 20 inches long, but this is very rare. As a general rule they are from 4–9 inches long, in the shape of an elongated oval. The ground colour is a rather yellowish-green that shades to a dark olive green along the margin. However, the ground colour is diversified by alternate large and small dark green blotches, springing from the midrib. These blotches look like the drawing of a tree in some primitive manuscript. The underside of the leaf is a deep claret colour. The leaves are quite tough and leathery and so will tolerate room conditions better than some of the more delicate species, some of which have even more attractive leaves.

Calathea louisae

The leaves are shorter and rounder than those of *C. insignis* and they do not have the very marked blotches that characterize the leaf of the former plant. Instead, there are patches of yellowish colour emanating from the midrib in a fairly regular pattern. The underside of the leaf has a purple tinge and a very marked dark green margin.

Calathea mackoyana (Peacock Plant)

This is rather less easy to keep in good condition than the other two, as the leaves are somewhat thinner. On the other hand, it is so exquisite that it is worth a little extra attention. The leaves are an elongated oval in shape and in bought plants will be about 6 inches long and 4 inches across. The upper side of the leaf has a medium green edge, but the ground colour of the leaf is silvery. This ground colour is diversified by dark green blotches in much the same way as the leaves of *C. insignis*, but on the underside these dark green blotches are rosy purple, and when seen against the light the blotches give out a rosy glow, while the silvery portion appears transparent. The compost in which this plant grows should be kept slightly moister than the other calatheas and there is always a risk of the leaves browning at the edge during the winter. If this happens they can be trimmed with nail scissors. The plant is sometimes sold under the name of *Maranta mackoyana*, but if you bear the second part of the name in mind you are sure of getting the real Mackoy.

Chlorophytum comosum variegatum (C)

One of the easiest and most indestructible of house-plants, this is often offered under the name of *Chlorophytum capense*, from which it differs by its habit of producing tufts of young plants at the ends of the flower stems. The plant has a fountain of bluebell-like leaves, about ¾ inch across and up to a foot long, which are ivory with narrow green margins. Like most variegated plants, this likes a well lit situation and should not be watered very frequently during the winter months. During the summer it will throw up what would be flowering stems in most plants, but in this case the flowers are replaced by tiny plants. If these are bent down and secured to the surface of some compost in another pot, by means of a hairpin or something similar, they will root into the soil, and, when well rooted, the stem can be cut and you have another plant. However, do not be in too great a hurry to sever the young plant from its parent; wait until you see that the leaves are at least 2 inches long. You can also increase the plants by division, but since large plants look so much more impressive than small ones do, it is probably better to encourage the plant to make a really large and imposing specimen. Well-grown plants are fairly greedy and need ample feeding in the summer and will also enjoy ample water between mid-May and mid-August.

Cissus antarctica (Kangaroo Vine) (C)

A climbing plant, supporting itself by means of tendrils, so that it will require some support, but otherwise one of the easiest of house-plants. The shining dark green leaves are about 4 inches long and 2 inches across and are roughly heart-shaped. The leaf stems are reddish in colour and contrast well. The plant is equally happy in sun or in shade and will tolerate gas and oil fumes. During the growing season the growing point can be nipped out, to encourage the growth of side-shoots and these can in turn can be stopped to encourage side-shoots on the side-shoots. With patience it is possible to get a very large plant, up to 8 feet high, but it is not necessary. Cuttings of one-year-old wood will generally root without difficulty. The young growth is usually too soft and will rot, although some people manage to root trails in water. The plant is not a particularly rapid grower, but should be potted on every two years.

Codiaeum variegatum pictum (Croton) (I, W)

These are shrubs belonging to the spurge family, and the whole plant is filled with a milky fluid (characteristic of this family) that spurts out if the leaves or stems are pierced in any way. The plants have most frequently oval leaves of varying sizes, but some are long and grass-like, while others are jagged, so it is not easy to give a general description. In the same way they show an enormous range of colouring, from the green speckled with yellow of 'Apple Leaf' to combinations of green, pink, orange and nearly black. They are thus extremely colourful and ornamental, but they are not the easiest of plants to keep in good condition. Draughts are particularly resented by them—they will shed their leaves in a draughty situation—and rapid changes of temperature will have the same result. Although most of the varieties do best under Warm conditions, they will do better under Intermediate conditions if the temperature is kept steady than they would do under Warm conditions that were subject to sudden changes of temperature. Given this unchanging temperature and freedom from draughts, they are not otherwise difficult. There is no objection to gradual changes in temperature, provided that they are not too extreme; it is the sudden change they dislike. The varieties with mainly green leaves and those with long narrow leaves will grow in

61

lower temperatures than the more ornamental, broader-leaved plants.

It is usual to pinch out the growing point of many house-plants in the spring to encourage them to make a bushy plant, but this should not be done with crotons. In the first place they do not bush out, and in the second the plant would be covered with the milky latex which would gush out when you removed the growing point. The plants need to be in a very well-lit position and they resent oil or gas fumes. During the growing-season they will require feeding. If you succeed with the plant and it becomes very leggy, it may be worth while to cut it down to within 8 inches of the ground and allow it to break again. Have cotton-wool available when you do this, so that you can mop up the milky latex before it hardens.

Cordyline terminalis (I)

These are low-growing shrubs with oblong-oval leaves that may be 12 inches long and are about 4 inches across. In time they can make quite tall shrubs, but they are slow growing and they are rarely more than 2 feet high in cultivation. They have leaves that are often a very vivid red or crimson when young and which fade to either a very dark purple or to a dark green as they age. Some varieties have leaves mottled with cream or white, and all the different kinds are extremely ornamental. These coloured leaves do not appear until the plants are a few years old, so they have to be grown on for this period in the nursery, which means that they are rather expensive.

They are not difficult plants to keep in good condition and though they thrive in Intermediate conditions, there is every reason to suppose that they would survive the winter under Cool conditions without damage. It is unfortunate that their price rather discourages experiment, but one of the writers kept a plant successfully through the winter in a cool green-house, where, on occasion, the temperature was as low as

40°F. Naturally, with these lower temperatures they have to be kept as dry as possible, but even under Intermediate conditions they will not require much water during the winter, although they will prove thirsty enough during the summer. Until people started growing them as house-plants, it was always assumed that they needed very warm conditions, but either the earlier gardeners were wrong or the plants have become acclimatized to cooler conditions. They require a rather rich compost and should be fed during the summer. They also like a well-lit situation, although direct sunshine can scorch the young leaves slightly and this should be guarded against. They do tolerate oil and gas fumes in moderation. The individual leaves are not extremely long-lived and you must expect some to fall in the summer, when the new ones are unfurling; they generally remain on the plant for two years. The plant is often sold under the name of *Dracaena terminalis*.

Cryptanthus (Earth Star) (C, I)

These dwarf plants belong to the same family, the *Bromeliadaceae*, as aechmea, but unlike the latter plant, do not have a 'vase' and so need watering in the usual manner. They are small and compact and are good plants for bottle gardens. In the wild they grow on rocks and have a very small root system, so that the provision of a moist atmosphere around them is of great importance. The species most frequently grown is *Cryptanthus tricolor*, which is one of the largest; the leaves can reach a length of 10 inches. These leaves are sword-shaped, with a pink margin and a centre variegated cream and dark green, and spread out in a flat rosette. Many other species are grown and they are all attractive. They differ in size and in leaf colour; some make rosettes only a few inches across, while others are nearly as large as *C. tricolor*. In some the leaves are banded, others are striped. Yet others have sword-shaped leaves coming to a point, or they may be strap-shaped with blunt ends, while *C. beuckeri* has leaves shaped like a teaspoon.

They all need similar treatment. This includes a well-lit situation, a moist atmosphere and no drying-out at the roots. However, in the winter, they will require very little water to keep them moist. During the winter the leaves lose some of their brilliance. This is apparently due to the short amount of daylight at that season and they soon recover their brilliant shades after the end of March. All the bromeliads appreciate fresh air and this should be provided whenever temperatures allow. The plants survive well under Cool conditions, but if warmer temperatures can be provided, they appreciate it. During the summer the plants produce rather inconspicuous white flowers; those in the centre of the plant are male flowers and only bear stamens, but later hermaphrodite flowers are produced from the leaf axils.

Dieffenbachia (Dumb Cane) (W)

These members of the arum family have large, oblong-oval leaves borne spirally around a central stem, that becomes trunk-like as the plant ages and also assumes a corkscrew shape. The leaves are green ornamented with blotches of yellow or cream according to the different species and varieties. They need as Warm conditions as can be provided and also revel in a moist atmosphere. They should not be allowed to dry out, although in winter water should be applied as infrequently as possible. The individual leaves are rather thin and not very long-lasting, but fresh leaves are produced in quantity during the growing season. They are greedy plants needing a rather rich compost and it may well be that they are not very suited for soilless composts. They should be placed in a shaded, but not dark position. A large number of different species are offered, mostly forms of *Dieffenbachia picta*, but the two species described have proved the most reliable for room work.

All plants of the arum family contain a very acrid juice, which has so ghastly a taste, that the risk of anyone being poisoned, through eating it, is minimal. The juice of one of the dieffenbachias, *D. seguine*, which is not in cultivation, has the reputation of causing temporary loss of speech, which accounts for its popular name of Dumb Cane. However, in spite of occasional alarmist reports, the grower need feel no nervousness with dieffenbachias or with any other member of the arum family. No one is liable to eat house-plants, in the first place, and in the second, if anyone was so ill-advised as to chew on a portion, the revolting flavour would make them desist long before any harm could be done.

Dieffenbachia amoena

This is a very large vigorous plant with leaves that can reach a foot in length and 5 inches across. The leaf is dark green with cream marbling along the principal lateral veins. This is somewhat tougher than most of the dumb canes and might well succeed in Intermediate conditions.

Dieffenbachia arvida 'Exotica'

This is a smaller plant than *D. amoena*, but much more brilliant. The leaves are about 6 inches long and 3 inches across and when they have just unfurled, they look like a small leaf of *D. amoena*. However, as they age, the cream marbling spreads over most of the leaf and there is considerably more cream than green in the mature leaf. This is probably the best of the dieffenbachias to try, as it is very rewarding and has proved itself tolerant of room conditions. They do not enjoy either gas or oil fumes.

Dracaena (Dragon Plant)

There are a large number of these grown and they do not all require the same treatment, as far as temperatures are conthe plant requires far less water during the winter, it will still take a certain amount and should not be allowed to become too dry at any time. Here again is a plant that will do well in the bottle garden for a time.

X Fatshedera lizei (C)

This is a bigeneric hybrid between the next plant, *Fatsia japonica* and the Irish ivy, *Hedera hibernica*. It was made in 1912 by the Lizé brothers, who had a nursery in Brittany. The resultant plant is undecided whether to be a shrub or a climber and has compromised by producing a long narrow stem that needs a cane as a support. The leaves are shaped like the pollen parent, *Fatsia japonica*, but are only about the same size as those of a largish ivy. There are three forms available. There is the type plant with plain, dark green leaves, which can be put out in the garden when it gets too large for the home. A second one is the variegated form, *F. l. variegata*, which has a broad, irregular cream margin to the leaves. This is very attractive, although a little more tender than the type, and with the annoying trait of browning slightly at the tips in the winter. The third is *F. l. undulata*, which has a green leaf with a wavy edge and is as hardy as the type. The green-leaved plants will grow in quite heavy shade, while the variegated form needs more light. The growing point can be taken out each spring to prevent the plants becoming too long and lanky, but the plant will not throw many side-shoots. The plant is kept reasonably moist, even during the winter, and takes quite a lot of water during the summer. It is practically trouble free, although it can be attacked by red spider if the atmosphere becomes too dry in the summer, and is unaffected by gas or by oil fumes. Cuttings of unripe wood are fairly easy to root.

Fatsia japonica (False Castor-oil Plant) (C)

As we have said, you may sometimes find this under the name

of *Aralia sieboldii*. This can be grown out of doors in many parts of the country and is one of those plants that will not relish warm conditions in the winter. The type has wide, palmately-lobed, dark green, shining leaves and can eventually make a large, shrubby bush up to 8 feet high with heads of ivy-like flowers in November. However, it is only used as a house-plant while it is of manageable proportions. Much more attractive is the variegated variety, in which the tips of the lobes are coloured ivory. These tips have an irritating habit of browning slightly in the winter and may have to be mani-cured. Otherwise the plant is trouble-free. The type will grow well in quite heavy shade, although this is not essential. The variegated form will need more light in order to bring the variegation well out. Fatsia is unaffected by gas or oil fumes.

Ficus

Quite a number of these are grown as house-plants, but they are so different in form and need so many different treatments that there can be no general directions given.

Ficus benjamina (I)

This is a quick-growing shrub, that could eventually make a large tree. It throws branches without any prompting in the way of stopping and gives a graceful weeping-willow effect. The leaves are oblong-oval in shape and end in a point; they are about 4 inches long and 1½ inches across and a soft green in colour. The plant will thrive in shady conditions, but has no objection to light. The leaves are very numerous and it is not easy to keep them free from dust, but you should attempt to do so. During the winter it is natural for the older leaves to turn yellow and drop off, so do not get alarmed when this happens. This is one of those plants that must never be allowed to become too dry although, should this happen, the plant wilts, so that remedial measures can quickly be provided. The plant the variegated forms, when the young leaves are emerging.

Ficus pumila (C)

It seems very difficult to think that this plant belongs to the same genus as the last. It forms a low, creeping shrub with wiry stems and small heart-shaped leaves, about an inch long and ½ inch across, which are set thickly all along the stems. The stems produce roots at intervals, by which they can support themselves in the same way that ivy does, and cuttings will easily root. It can be grown as a trailer or as a climber. Like ivy, the plant will eventually produce fruiting branches with differently-shaped, much larger, leaves but these branches do not carry aerial roots. However, the house-plant grower is not likely to see these, as the plant has to become very large before they are produced. In exceptionally favoured districts on the west coast, the plant has been grown out of doors, so it will thrive in Cool conditions. It is suitable for bottle gardens, when small, but may eventually grow rather large for these. The plant should have shady conditions and will grow in very dark situations. It will not tolerate direct sunlight. This is one of the few plants which should never be allowed to dry out and the compost should be kept moist at all times. It does not care for gas fumes. Although the individual leaves are small, they are produced so copiously that the stems are well-nigh invisible. At one time there was a variegated form of this ficus, but it proved disappointing as the plant invariably reverted to the plain green-leaved form.

Ficus radicans variegata (I)

This is in many ways similar to *F. pumila* in habit, as it has the same tendency to produce roots at every leaf joint. The leaves are larger, up to 2½ inches long and 1 inch across and they are lance-shaped, tapering to a point. They are dark green with cream margins. Although somewhat more attractive than *F.*

pumila it requires warmer conditions and a better-lit situation. Again, it should never be allowed to dry out and the compost should always be moist. During the winter it is not improbable that some leaves may be discoloured. If this happens the plant can be cut back in the spring. Both this plant and the preceding one will produce side-shoots without the necessity of nipping the growing-points out, but stopping will encourage their production. This plant, perhaps, is more suitable for the bottle garden than *F. pumila*, as, although it will in time become too large, it will take considerably longer to do so. However, Intermediate conditions are essential and so, too, is a moist atmosphere.

Hedera (Ivy) (C)

The ivies supply a large number of easily-grown house-plants, but the forms of *Hedera helix* insist on low winter temperatures and should only be grown under Cool conditions. *H. canariensis*, although equally happy under these conditions, will tolerate the warmth of Intermediate temperatures, which the forms of *H. helix* will not. The plants present no difficulties; the green-leaved forms will grow in shade, which may be heavy, while the variegated forms need rather more light.

Hedera canariensis foliis variegatis (Canary Ivy) (C, I)

This is a climbing ivy and must be given the support of canes or something similar. It is a slow grower in pots, although it will ramp away if planted out of doors, and generally two or three plants are put into each pot. The leaves are roughly triangular in shape with a grey-green centre and a cream-coloured margin. The amount of cream and green varies from leaf to leaf and no leaf is identical with its neighbours. Coming from the Canary Islands, the plant will tolerate quite dry conditions and excessive water will cause the leaves to yellow and fall. Yearly stopping seems to make a more vigorous plant, although inches across, and in the unvariegated form are a pleasant, rather bright, green. The variegated form has leaves almost entirely cream-coloured when young, but as they age, the cream portion is confined to the margins. 'Chicago' is rather liable to revert to the unvariegated form, and any unvariegated shoots should be removed. Lack of light also seems to inhibit the variegation and during the winter most of the leaves will be plain green. If the shoots are pruned back to the first well-variegated leaf in the spring, the new growths will probably be of the right type. Cuttings of all these ivies are generally taken in May.

Hedera 'Eva'. This is a fascinating plant in which the leaves are continually changing colour. Moreover, one plant will bear leaves of different shapes. The most frequently seen is a 3-lobed leaf, with the central lobe at least twice the length of the side lobes, but sometimes one of these lobes is nearly as large as the central lobe, which gives the leaf an oddly asymmetric appearance; on the other hand, sometimes the leaf is practically unlobed and appears diamond-shaped. The young leaves are almost entirely ivory in colour, but as they age, the green portions increase and the old leaves are almost entirely green with a slight mottling of a paler green. It is not self-branching and is a very slow grower. The individual leaves are very small. This ivy sometimes appears with the name 'Little Eva'.

Hedera 'Fantasia'. Here again we have an ivy the leaves of which become progressively greener as they age. The leaves generally have a cream-coloured margin, but some are blotched all over. They are comparatively large, about 3 inches long and as much across, and are 5-lobed, in the usual ivy-leaf shape. The plant is fairly vigorous, but is not self-branching.

Hedera 'Glacier'. Not a self-branching ivy, but one that produces side-shoots in moderation quite early. The leaves are a rather odd shade of silvery-grey with a cream margin, which tends to disappear as the leaves age. The leaf stalks are an attractive purple shade and, if the plant is placed in full light, the leaves themselves take on a purplish hue. This is a splendid plant if you need a trailer, as it falls most gracefully. The leaves are medium-sized and 3-lobed.

Hedera 'Green Ripple'. A fascinating aspect of many of the ivies is the way that the leaf shapes change as the leaf develops. This is especially marked in this variety. All the leaves are characterized by a very long, thin central lobe which is half the length of the entire leaf, but the young leaves have only three lobes, so that the leaf consists of a long central lobe and the two short side lobes. However, as the leaf matures, these side lobes become lobed themselves and the fully mature leaf has five lobes, although the basic impression of a long, thin leaf is preserved the whole time.

The plant is self-branching, with leaves that are bright green when young, but darken as they age. It is advisable to stop the main growing-point from time to time during the summer, as it is rather liable to throw a lot of stem, without many leaves to clothe it, and the stopping encourages a more vigorous growth of side-shoots.

Hedera 'Heisse'. This could briefly be described as a self-branching 'Glacier'. The leaves are about the same size, 2 inches long and 2 inches across, but they are 5-lobed. They are similar in colour to those of 'Glacier', though the cream margin is slightly more persistent. If an upright plant is needed with silvery-grey leaves, this is the best variety.

Hedera 'Little Diamond'. This little charmer has very small, unlobed, diamond-shaped leaves that are only 1 inch long and barely $\frac{1}{2}$ an inch across. As the leaves age they become a little larger and broaden out slightly. The colour is grey-green with an ivory margin, but the ground colour is less silvery than in the two varieties, 'Glacier' and 'Heisse'. This is a self-branching ivy and tends to grow rather slowly. As a general rule ivies grow too rapidly for bottle gardens, but if you did want to insert one, 'Little Diamond' would be one of the best to choose.

Hedera 'Lutzii'. This is a self-branching ivy with a great number of small leaves that are basically 3-lobed, although the side lobes are slightly indented. The leaves are mottled with varying shades of pale green that tend towards a pale yellow and have rather an unhealthy appearance to some eyes. Others, however, find this mottling remarkably attractive, so the only thing to do is to have a look and decided for yourself. The plant makes a neat, twiggy little bush, which will stand without support. It grows at a reasonable rate, but not very rapidly.

Hedera 'Maculata'. This is probably a variety of the Irish ivy, *H. hibernica* and has larger leaves than the varieties of *H. helix*. These leaves are 3-lobed, about 4 inches long and as much across, borne on attractive purplish-pink stems. They are a medium green, heavily mottled with creamy-yellow when young, but this cream mottling tends to fade out as the leaf ages and the bottom leaves are a dark green with very little mottling. The plant is not self-branching and needs to be supported with a cane or something similar. It grows rather slowly in a pot, although it will grow rapidly if planted out of doors against a wall.

The ten varieties we have described are the most popular of the ivies that are being grown at present, but it does not exhaust the list of those that are available, and new ones are constantly being introduced.

Hoya carnosa variegata (Wax Plant) (C, I)

This will eventually make quite a vigorous climber or trailer, but growth is rather slow in the early stages. If given a stake to ascend, it will twine round it. It requires a fairly rich soil and a semi-shaded position. The leaves are thick and fleshy, which indicates that short periods of drought can be tolerated. This helps to minimize the risk of overwatering in the winter. There are two forms with variegated leaves. That most frequently seen has a dark green centre and a cream margin, which is pink in the early stages; the rarer variety has a golden centre to the leaf and a dark green margin. The individual leaves are oblong-oval in shape, about 3 inches long and 1½ inches across. The plant has an unusual habit of growth. The new stem will elongate to its full extent, before any of the new leaves start to unfurl. This gives an appearance which is rather alarming to those who do not know its strange habit. The mature leaves are in the centre of the plant, from which stems like bootlaces emerge in the early summer. However, do not be alarmed. Once the stem has completed its growth, the new leaves will unfurl and enlarge quite satisfactorily. In the green-house the plant will eventually bear umbels of star-shaped, waxy, fragrant flowers, but these are not produced until the plant is quite large and they are not likely to be seen in the home. The plant will survive happily under Cool conditions, but will grow more rapidly in the Intermediate section. Hoyas resent any interference with their growth and they should not be stopped or pruned in any way. If a temperature of 65°F can be provided, cuttings that are firm but not woody will root quite rapidly.

Hypocyrta glabra (Clog Plant) (I)

An attractive dwarf, shrubby plant which will grow to about 6 inches high, but which can be 12 inches, or even more, across. Its stems are covered with rather fleshy, elliptic leaves of a bright shining green. From the axils of these the flowers emerge. These have a pale orange calyx, from which the waxy, orange, red-tipped, tubular flowers protrude. These darken to nearly scarlet when they age. The individual flowers are not very large, but are produced in numbers over a long period. They are produced on the current year's growth, so it is as well to give all the branchlets a slight prune in April to encourage side-shoots to develop and also to prevent the plant carrying too many old, non-flowering branches. In the greenhouse the plants are given semi-shaded conditions, but in the home they can be put in a well-lit situation. Their fleshy leaves mean that they can be kept on the dry side during cold periods without any ill effect and at no time do they require excessive water, which could cause the flower buds to drop off (so, too, can excessive dryness). As the plant comes from Brazil, Intermediate conditions appear called for, but they would probably do reasonably well under Cool conditions. If a little heat is available, cuttings will root quite easily.

Impatiens petersiana (C, I)

This is very similar to the popular Busy Lizzie (*Impatiens holstii*), but can be distinguished by its leaves. These are longer than those of Busy Lizzie and deep purple in colour. It bears the same brilliant red flowers in equal profusion. This is not a plant that one normally wants to keep for very long, as it will eventually get rather leggy and less floriferous. Cuttings root very easily in the spring and summer; they will even root if the tips are just placed in water and it is as well to root a few cuttings yearly. Under Cool conditions many of the leaves will fall during the winter and the plant will not look very attractive but, if cut back, it will break away well in the spring. Young plants should be stopped a couple of times to encourage the formation of a good bushy plant, and a well-lit situation is essential. Gas fumes cause some leaf drop, but are not fatal to the plant. As the plant is seldom kept for more than 18 months, it is one that soilless compost will suit very well, especially since plants appear to make a more rapid initial growth in these composts. This is a striking plant with its purple leaves and crimson flowers, and one that is agreeably easy to grow.

17. *Ficus radicans variegata*

18. *Hedera canariensis foliis variegatis*

19. *Hedera* 'Maculata'

20. *Impatiens
petersiana*

21. *Maranta*
leuconeura
kerchoveana

22. *Monstera pertusa*

23. *Neoregelia carolinae tricolor*

24. *Pandanus
veitchii*

25. *Peperomia*
   hederaefolia

26. *Peperomia magnoliaefolia*

27. *Philodendron hastatum*

28. *Philodendron scandens*

29. *Pilea cadierei nana*

30. *Platycerium alcicorne*

31. *Saintpaulia ionantha*

32. *Senecio macroglossus variegatus*

33. *Spathiphyllum wallisii*

34. *Tradescantia* 'Rochford's Quicksilver'

It should never be allowed to dry out, although watering should be reduced to the minimum in winter under Cool conditions.

Maranta leuconeura (I, W)

Marantas are closely related to the Calatheas and need very similar treatment: shade and a warm, moist atmosphere. They are, however, much lower growing and make a more spreading plant. They seem to be very variable, and at least three named varieties are offered for sale. They all require the same treatment, but differ in size and in leaf shape. The smallest of the three is *Maranta leuconeura massangeana*. This has elliptic leaves that are up to 4 inches long and 2½ inches across. The ground colour is a rather soft lawn green. The midrib and the lateral veins are picked out in white to give a herring-bone effect. The portion of the leaf between the lateral veins is a darker green than the margin.

A second variety is *M. l. kerchoveana*, slightly larger, with leaves up to 5 inches long and 3½ inches across. Young leaves are emerald green with red blotches between the lateral veins, but both the green and the red darken with age to a dark green and maroon.

The variety *M. l. erythrophylla*, which is usually sold under the name *M. l. tricolor*, is the largest and most spectacular. The leaves may exceed 6 inches in length, but are not much wider than those of *M. l. kerchoveana*. In this plant the lateral veins are a dark crimson and there are dark green blotches stemming from the midrib between them. The remainder of the leaf is a yellowish-green.

If they are given the conditions of warmth, shade and a moist atmosphere that they would have naturally, these marantas will grow very vigorously and will need repotting yearly. Like their relatives, the calatheas, they should never be exposed to direct sunlight. They are extremely suitable for bottle gardens, where they can spread unchecked. They will take as much food

F   81

as is sensible to give during the growing season, from mid-May to the end of August. However, they will only grow vigorously when the temperature is 65°F or over, so that in the event of the summer being chilly, they will not need such frequent feeding.

Monstera pertusa (C, I)

This is usually sold under the name of *Monstera deliciosa borsigiana*, which is a horrible mouthful, besides being inaccurate. It is one of several climbing plants of the arum family, which are characterized by producing aerial roots at every leaf-joint. The monsteras are also notable for the curious perforations that occur in the adult leaves. It is thought that this is to give the large leaves protection in high winds. The plant grows horizontally in the wild and must be tied to a stake if it is wanted in an upright form. The aerial roots can be trained down to enter the soil in the pot in small specimens, but as the stem elongates, this will not be possible. Juvenile leaves are heart-shaped, but as the plant develops, the leaves become larger and develop first the deeply serrated edges, and finally the curious perforations that are so typical of the genus. A mature leaf is up to 12 inches long and 10 inches across. If a mature plant is placed in very deep shade, it will not produce these typical leaves, but those of the juvenile plant, just heart-shaped and entire, so that in order to get the best effects, they should be placed in a fairly well-lit situation.

Watering is a matter of some delicacy. They should not be allowed to dry out, but excessive damp will cause the leaves to turn yellow or to turn brown at the tips. The plant over-winters happily in Cool conditions, but a temperature of 65°F is necessary before any growth will take place, so they should be placed in a warm room during the summer. It is possible to grow a very large plant in time, if you so desire. In the late spring you can chop off the growing tip with a mature leaf and pot this up to root and give you an additional plant. It may be some little time before the old plant will break again, and it should be kept fairly dry until the new shoot is seen. This is a greedy plant and if not fed well the leaves will not attain their full dimensions. Gas and oil fumes are tolerated, but not enjoyed.

Neanthe bella (Dwarf Palm) (C)

Also sometimes known as *N. elegans*, or *Chamaedorea elegans*, this is a tiny, slow-growing palm, with feathery leaves that are about 8 inches long. The individual leaflets on each leaf may be 4 inches long, but are only 1 inch wide and are elliptic in shape. This is an easy plant, which will do quite well in the bottle garden and is useful in mixed groups. Older leaves are larger and less graceful. The plant can be kept rather dry during the winter without ill effects but, naturally, this should not be overdone and it requires little feeding during the summer. Indeed, a rather meagre diet seems to suit it best. It will tolerate a drier atmosphere than many other plants and does not seem to be affected by gas or by oil fumes. A fairly well-lit situation seems to be the most suitable, but it will thrive in light shade and is altogether a plant whose needs are easy to satisfy.

Neoregelia carolinae tricolor (I)

This is another of the epiphytic bromeliads and is not likely ever to need repotting. It will form in time a large, flat rosette, up to 2 feet across and the sword-shaped leaves may be as long as 15 inches, although rarely more than 1 inch across. Like the aechmea (see p. 50), the plant has a vase in its centre which should be kept full of water. If rain water is obtainable, it is certainly to be preferred and during the winter it is advisable to see that it has reached room temperature before adding it to the water already present. The long narrow leaves have the centre striped with deep cream and pale pink, which fades to an ivory as the leaf ages, so that mature leaves are green, deep cream and ivory. Just before the flowers are due to appear the plant will produce shorter, broader leaves that are a vivid crimson in colour and which are far more conspicuous than the flowers themselves. These are light blue in colour and barely emerge from the water in the vase, where they look like miniature water-lilies, half an inch across. After flowering is over, the plant slowly dies, although there may well be some side-shoots to grow on. It is best, therefore, to buy a fairly young plant, so that you can enjoy the variegated leaves and the later crimson leaves for some time. The plant should be put in a semi-shaded, but not dark, position. Too dark a situation would inhibit the variegation, but direct sunlight is unwelcome in excess. An occasional short exposure will do no harm.

Nephthytis 'Emerald Gem' (Goose-foot Plant) (I)

The correct name for this plant is *Syngonium podophyllum* and why people should find nephthytis easier to say than syngonium is curious. This is a climber belonging to the arum family, very similar to the popular philodendrons to which we shall shortly be coming. Like them, it produces aerial roots at each leaf-joint, and will do best if it can be trained on to cork bark or on to a wire cylinder that has been filled with moss. If this is done you must take the necessary trouble to see that the bark or moss is kept moist, so that the aerial roots can absorb some nourishment. The plant will grow adequately enough if trained to an ordinary cane, but the bark or moss does help to produce larger leaves and more luxuriant growth.

The young leaves are shaped like an arrow-head, but when the plant is more mature, the bottom lobes of the arrow-head become themselves shaped like an arrow-head, so that you get a leaf that can be divided into three sections: the central lobe, which may be 7 inches long and the two side lobes, which are about half this size, but which are splayed out, so that the base of the leaf measures 7 inches across. The ground colour of this leaf is a dark green, but the midrib and the main lateral veins are zoned with a lighter green (not emerald green in spite of its name), so that the leaf has a variegated effect, which is rather quiet in its appeal.

The plant does best in shady conditions, but these should not be too dark, and it has no objection to a well-lit situation. Plenty of moisture is required in the growing season and a moist atmosphere is desirable; during the winter nephthytis are best kept on the dry side, like the majority of house-plants. They like a rich compost and plenty of feeding in the summer. They will tolerate gas and oil fumes.

Pandanus veitchii (Screw-pine) (I, W)

The pandanus get their odd name of screw-pines from the fact that their leaves are thought to resemble those of a pineapple while, in mature plants, the trunks are corkscrew-shaped. They are slow-growing plants, however, and these trunks are rarely seen in the greenhouse and never in house-plants.

Pandanus veitchii has leaves up to 18 inches long, although only a few inches across, which are sword-shaped, and dark green with silver margins. The edges are sometimes slightly toothed. The plants do require plenty of warmth and will do best under Warm conditions, although they will be satisfactory under Intermediate temperatures, even though they will not grow very rapidly. Provided the warmth is there, they are very easy to keep in good condition and they will do quite well in a dry atmosphere. They like ample water during the summer and should not be allowed to dry out in the winter although, as always, the amount should be much reduced during this period. We would imagine this would be a plant for which soilless composts would not prove suitable, as they are only potted-on at long intervals and so need a compost that is full of nourishment. There seems to be no record of their reaction to gas fumes, but from the appearance of the plant, one would expect them to be tolerant.

Peperomia (I)

There are a large number of these small, attractively-leaved plants that are grown as house-plants. Most of them have rather fleshy leaves, which means that they will tolerate periods of drought if necessary. Indeed, in the wild one may see them so shrivelled up that one would think they would never recover, yet directly after a shower they have plumped out again. They tend, in the wild, to grow in the moss at the base of trees and they have a very small root system; they are practically epiphytic. They all like shady conditions and a moist atmosphere during the growing season and they can be expected to thrive in soilless composts. Since they never make very large plants they are ideal for bottle gardens although, as they are rather brittle, it is not easy to insert them without some damage. However, they can soon make this damage good. They will need potting-on at very rare intervals but should be fed, although not excessively, during the summer. In the late summer some of the species will throw small white, spiky, inflorescences, which are attractive, although not showy.

The house-plant peperomias come in two forms: those that throw all their leaves on longish stalks from the root and those that have a more shrubby constitution and bear their leaves on short stalks, all along the main stem, which will also branch. Those in the first section are liable to rot in the centre if overwatered and care should be taken that too much water does not lodge in the centre of the plant. There is much to be said for watering them from below, by standing the pots in a bowl of water, the level of which does not come higher than the pots, and leaving them there until the soil surface appears moist.

The most popular species that come from a central growing-point are *Peperomia caperata*, *P. hederaefolia* and *P. sandersii* (*P. argyreia*).

Peperomia caperata only grows about 3 inches high and has large numbers of heart-shaped leaves, which are not more than 1¼ inches long. The surface of these leaves is very corrugated and they are a very dark green in colour with a purple tinge in the vallies of the corrugation, while the peaks have a greyish colour. The stalks are pale pink, but the leaves are so thickly set that the stalks are not visible. The mousetail-like in-florescences are a very pure white and are sometimes branched, so as to give an antler-like appearance. If a leaf with its stalk is pulled from the root, it will itself root and produce another plant if the temperature is around 65°F, which it often is in the summer. When first introduced into this country, the plant was liable to a virus attack which gave distorted leaves. This seems to have been rogued out but, should it reappear, the plants should be destroyed.

Peperomia hederaefolia is rather like a larger edition of *P. caperata*. It has the same heart-shaped leaves, but they may be 2½ inches long and 2 inches across and the leaves are not deeply corrugated, but only slightly undulating, so that the leaf looks as though quilted. The colour is a pale grey for the most part, but the areas along the principal veins are a dark olive green. The plant makes its best effect in a mixed group. Propagation is similar to that for *P. caperata*, but take care to insert the base of the stem only a very little way into the peat and sand mixture. It is not necessary to use the whole stalk; it can be cut at half its length. If inserted too deeply, the new young leaves rot before they emerge.

Peperomia sandersii is the popular 'rugby football plant' and is the handsomest of all the peperomias. As the name implies, the leaves are shaped like a rugby football and are silver in colour, with dark green bands along the principal veins. A well-grown leaf is 4 inches long and 3 inches across. The stalks are dark red. The plant is very sensitive to draughts and is liable to rot if overwatered; it is altogether more touchy than the other peperomias. They will all tolerate gas and oil fumes in moderation. It is propagated by cutting the leaf in half and just inserting the cut surface in the propagating medium, when plantlets will appear at the ends of the main veins. Without a greenhouse it is a matter of some delicacy to bring these plantlets on to a good size and if you succeed you can congratulate yourself. The correct name of this plant is *P. argyreia*, but you are not likely to find it being offered under this name.

The most popular shrubby peperomias are *P. magnoliaefolia* and *P. obtusifolia*. *P. magnoliaefolia* is offered in two variegated forms. The one most frequently seen produces a young leaf which is almost entirely ivory, with a thin grey-green streak in the centre. As the leaf ages, this green portion takes over from the ivory and the older leaves are almost entirely green. In the form known as 'Green Gold', the variegation is more persistent and is also rather more yellow, and the plant has larger leaves. In the commoner form the leaves, which are oval in shape, are about 2 inches long and 1¾ inches across; in 'Green Gold' you can add half an inch to each measurement. The young stem is reddish and fades to a green ornamented with red spots. The plants break naturally, but stopping in the spring will encourage side-shoots to form. Propagation is by stem cuttings, which should not be too soft.

Peperomia obtusifolia is the largest of the house-plant peperomias and can make a much-branched plant a foot high. The leaves are thick and fleshy, elliptic in shape and dark green with a purple edge. The stem is the same dark purple colour. This plant needs a better-lit situation than most of the other peperomias and will also tolerate lower temperatures. Indeed, it may be said that both the shrubby species described here like ample light and will thrive at a winter temperature of

50°F. Again propagation is by stem cuttings. The long mouse-tails are produced fairly freely in the autumn. The plant will branch without any encouragement in the way of stopping and this is the only species that may need potting-on every two years.

Philodendron

This, one of the most popular genera of house-plants, includes both climbers and herbaceous species. They will all thrive in Intermediate conditions, but two will also tolerate Cool conditions. Like the other members of the arum family we have discussed, the climbing species produce aerial roots at every leaf-joint and, ideally, should be trained on to bark or green wood, or up wire cylinders that are filled with moss. The idea is that the aerial roots penetrate these substances and obtain nourishment, as they would in the wild. In practice it is not at all easy to keep these supports sufficiently moist to be of any use in the home. It is easy enough in the greenhouse to syringe them rather heavily, but in the home you are liable to damage the furniture if you do this and it is easier to train them up a cane or some wire trellis. This means that the plants are more dependent on their terrestrial roots than wild plants would be, so they should be fed well during the growing season. They appreciate a moist atmosphere and this should be provided, both by plunging the pots in some absorbent matter that is kept damp, and also by spraying the leaves with a scent spray or something similar that will moisten the leaves without causing damage to your walls or furniture. In the U.S.A. *Philodendron scandens* is known as the bathroom plant, as it is so often put in that room where it revels in the steam.

Philodendron bipinnatifidum (C, I)

This is the only non-climbing species that we shall be discussing. As might be guessed from its name, the leaves are bipinnatifid. That means that the leaves are divided into numerous sections, but not into separate leaflets, and that these sections are themselves divided. This adds up to an extremely jagged leaf, which is basically arrow-head shaped. The plant can eventually grow extremely large, when it will carry leaves that are 2 feet long and 18 inches across, on stems themselves 18 inches long, so a full-grown plant is a massive affair. The plant is not a particularly rapid grower, and you will be able to keep a specimen for several years before you have a space problem. It is generally sold in a 5-inch pot, when the leaves are probably about 10 inches long and 8 inches across and the whole plant is about a foot high. The plant has only a single growing-point, from which the leaves spring. The new leaf is sheathed in the base of the stalk of the last leaf to have appeared, with the result that all the leaf-stalks have a boat-shaped hollow at their base, in which, originally, the next leaf to appear had been protected. The leaves of seedlings and young plants are heart-shaped and it is only when they are two years old that the fimbriations begin and they become more and more incised as the plant develops.

This philodendron can be grown under Cool conditions, although it will prefer the warmer Intermediate temperatures. It will tolerate gas and oil fumes. The plant is greedy, needing a rich, quick-draining compost and ample feeding during the growing-season. During the winter it should not be allowed to dry out completely, although watering should be as scant as possible; it can be repotted each spring, if it is growing vigorously. There is always a slight risk of the insect pest scale on the underside of the leaves, and they should be examined periodically. The plant is equally happy in sun or in shade and will even grow, albeit not too happily, in rather dark positions. In the course of years it will produce a short trunk, but it is a long time before this happens. Where a large plant is needed, you cannot do better than use this philodendron.

Philodendron erubescens 'Burgundy' (I)

This is a rather vigorous, large-leaved climber, needing as moist an atmosphere as you can provide. The leaves are shaped like an arrow-head, usually from 7–9 inches long, although they can reach a foot in length and, when mature, a very dark green, nearly black, with a purple underside. Since the surface is shining, the lower leaves give off purple reflections from the undersides of the upper leaves. The stems and leaf stalks are a rich wine-red, presumably a Burgundy red, so that the whole plant is a brilliant gamut of colours from Burgundy red to nearly black. Once it is well-established, the top can be cut off in the late spring and potted-up to root and make another plant. The original plant will break to give two or more growing points so that, eventually, a fairly bushy plant is created. The plant does not need repotting very often, but must be fed in summer, after the first season. It grows well in shady situations, but they should not be too dark. Gas and oil fumes are tolerated. This is, again, a delightful plant, but it is rather large and might take up too much room in a small room.

Philodendron hastatum (I)

Although it lacks the colours of *P. erubescens*, this is the best of the large-leaved climbing philodendrons to grow, where a large plant is not required. The shining, green leaves are shaped like a spear-head and are up to 7 inches long and 4 inches across at their base. The plant is not a very rapid grower. It has very broad, fleshy, leaf-stalks, which seems to suggest that it has to go through periods of drought in the wild. In the home it is kept moist and a moist atmosphere should also be provided if possible. During the winter, it can be kept on the dry side without ill effects, although it should not be left very dry for too long a period. It is, however, safe to let the soil dry out between waterings. If it should be in a soilless compost, this is

91

best not allowed to dry out completely, as it is difficult to re-moisten it. If this should happen, the pot should be immersed in a bucket of water and left there until bubbles no longer rise to the surface. The pot should then be removed and the compost firmed around the edges of the pot, as it is there that the compost shrinks, with the result that the water runs straight through without moistening the compost at all. A shady situation suits this plant best, but it should not be too dark, otherwise the leaves will be small and the growth will become thin and lank. The plant is tolerant of oil and gas fumes. The top can be removed to make another plant, but this philodendron grows best if it is not stopped. It is not a rapid grower.

Philodendron scandens (Sweetheart Vine) (C, I)

This is the easiest of all the climbing philodendrons and is one of the most popular of house-plants. The leaf is heart-shaped, about 4 inches long and 2½ inches across, and dark green in colour. The plant is a fairly vigorous climber and benefits from a yearly stopping, which will encourage a bushy growth. In any case the growth that is produced during the winter tends to be rather spindly and the leaves to be undersized, so it is worth while cutting the tip off, back to the first good leaf, in the spring. The tip you have removed can be rooted, but it is not a good idea to start a plant with a bad cutting and if you want to increase your stock, it is better to take cuttings later, when the leaves are the proper size and the growth is close-jointed.

As you continue to grow your philodendron you may find that the plant is getting taller than you require. If this happens, you can detach the plant from its support and fold it firmly in half, so that the growing tip is now down at the pot level. It will start to grow upwards again immediately, but you have halved its original height and you will also have a bushier plant. This bending of the plant is best done in the spring. The plant can be stopped immediately afterwards, so that you get your new growths coming from the base of the plant, where they are most needed. In theory this halving of the plant can go on indefinitely, but in practice it is probably simplest to cut the whole plant well back, once it has got too tall the second time. It will be well-rooted and will not take long to regenerate.

A rather shady position suits this plant best and it will survive in dark corners, although the leaves will not be at their best in these positions. Since all the members of the arum family that are grown as house-plants have thick, fleshy roots, it is essential that they should have a very quick-draining compost, as a waterlogged condition would soon cause the roots to rot. If this is provided, the plant will prove remarkably easy to grow and quite indifferent to gas or oil fumes. It is somewhat greedy and can scarcely be overfed.

Pilea cadierei nana (Aluminium Plant) (C, I)

The original *Pilea cadierei* was introduced to cultivation from Annam in Indo-China as recently as 1938. Since it will do quite well under cool conditions, it may be presumed to grow in the mountains in that tropical region. The leaves are an oblong-oval in shape, up to 3 inches long and 1½ inches across. They are dark green with patches of silver in the portions between the principal veins. If the plant becomes starved, the leaves tend to lose this silvery colour.

The original introduction tended to make a rather leggy untidy plant and had to be stopped twice yearly to keep it looking compact and bushy. However, the variety *nana* has now replaced this rather unsatisfactory type. In this variety the growth remains compact and bushy and the plant is not only more handsome, but also less trouble. It is still quite a good idea to nip out the growing-points in the spring as this will improve the appearance of the plants; the new leaves will have particularly good markings. The type has been replaced in commerce by the variety, but there may still be plants of the bad form around, as they were easy to keep going and to propagate, so if you are offered plants by friends, it is as well to inspect them tactfully.

The variety *nana* (the Latin for dwarf) makes a very suitable plant for bottle gardens, but the original introduction would eventually make too leggy a plant for such a position.

The plants thrive in a moderately shady position, but will also enjoy a well-lit situation. They require regular feeding during the growing season. They should not be allowed to dry out at any time and the soil should be kept moist even during the winter although, unless your rooms are very warm, they will only need watering at long intervals. They will tolerate gas and oil fumes, but they do not like them. Cuttings will root easily in the summer months and are best taken about mid-May.

Platycerium alcicorne (syn. **P.bifurcatum**) (Elk's-horn Fern) (C,I)

It has been a great surprise to find that this exotic-looking fern should grow so easily in the home. Most of the elk's-horn ferns need considerable heat and a very humid atmosphere, but this one will thrive under Cool conditions and in quite dry situations. In nature it is an epiphyte, growing on the trunks of trees, so that the pot should be canted at an angle and not put in the usual position, except when the plant is being watered.

This fern produces two sorts of leaves. At the base are large circular, rather shapeless leaves, which will girdle the pot and which, in the wild, cling to the tree trunk. From these arise the antler-shaped fronds that give the plants their popular name. As the plant ages the fronds of both sorts become ever larger and a well-grown, old plant may have fronds 2 feet long.

Although it is best to keep the compost continually moist, if it does become dry, the plant will quickly recover, even though it may have dried out completely and the fronds look withered.

Should such a disaster occur, place the plant in a bucket of water and leave it there for a few hours, after which the plant will be perfectly all right again. Far from objecting to gas and oil fumes, this fern seems to thrive in their presence. One of the best plants we know is situated just next to a gas cooker that is in frequent use.

Since the roots serve more for anchorage than for anything else, the actual composition of the compost is not of great importance, provided that it is one that will drain rapidly, and plants would do well in soilless cultures. They can be secured to portions of cork bark, by means of wire and will grow in these positions well in the greenhouse. This is not satisfactory in the home, owing to the difficulty of keeping them adequately supplied with water under these conditions. In the greenhouse they can be syringed several times a day. If the pot is placed in the usual position, that is to say, upright, the plant will not thrive. The main risk seems to be that water is liable to lodge in the centre of the fronds and cause the plant to rot. If the pot is put in some container, where it can be set at an angle, the plant will do better and will, indeed, give no difficulty at all. The pot must be stood upright while being watered, but once this has been finished, it should be replaced in its original position.

This is a plant that looks very effective if it is placed on some wall bracket or similar container, which will give the impression that the plant is growing out of the wall. The fronds are covered with a greyish bloom which is destroyed when the leaves are sprayed. So this, with *Senecio macroglossus*, is one of the few house-plants whose leaves should not be sprayed.

A fairly shady position suits this plant best and too much direct sunlight would not be liked. Since the plant can only be propagated by means of spores (which act in the place of the seeds of less primitive plants) it is only small plants that can be purchased for a reasonable figure. Large plants are many years old and have to be priced accordingly. However, they can be kept growing well in the home for many years without difficulty and probably only need repotting once every five years.

Rhoicissus rhomboidea (Natal Vine) (C, I)

This is a fairly vigorous plant that climbs by means of tendrils. The leaves are composed of three leaflets. The centre leaflet is about 4 inches long and $2\frac{1}{2}$ inches across, while the two lateral leaflets are slightly smaller. The young leaves are brownish in colour and somewhat hairy, but they mature to a dark, shining, green. The plant is tolerant of most conditions, although excessive sunshine might damage the young growth. The plant should be stopped every spring to encourage a bushy growth and with a large specimen it is advisable to be quite tough in shortening the growths, unless you require a very large plant.

Cuttings of fairly hard new growth will generally root very easily, sometimes they will root just by being placed in water. Gas and oil fumes appear to cause no damage. Growths that are too soft will not root, but will rot off, so do not be in too much of a hurry to take your cuttings.

Saintpaulia ionantha (African Violet) (I, W)

The beauty of these plants lies in their flowers more than in their leaves, although there are some varieties whose leaves are quite attractive in themselves. Unfortunately these varieties tend to flower rather less freely than those with the normal dark green, heart-shaped leaves. Although the African violet is one of the most popular of house-plants, it would be trifling with the truth to suggest that their successful cultivation in the home is particularly easy.

The points you want to aim for when growing this plant are: a humid atmosphere, a shady, but not dark, position and a temperature around 55°F at night and somewhat higher during the daytime—70°F is the recommended temperature. Since the plants are not very large and only a few inches high, there is no trouble in organizing the moist atmosphere. The pot is simply placed in a container containing some absorbent material, peat, vermiculite, moss, even old newspaper, which is kept moist at all times. There is also a lot to be said in favour of standing the pot on pebbles and allowing water to a depth of half an inch to be permanently at the base of these pebbles.

The watering of the actual soil is a process that requires some care. If the water is too cold, the roots get chilled and this causes the leaves to acquire unsightly white blotches. These not only look nasty, but also weaken the plant. What you should do is to water always with water at the same temperature, and the best temperatures seem to be those between 55 and 60°F. If you are keeping your room at the temperature we have suggested, your simplest method of getting the water to the right temperature is to store it in your room. It will reach the required temperature about 12 hours after being taken from the tap, so that if you keep your store of water filled up, you will always have water at the right temperature. If this is too much nuisance, you can always mix cold and hot water from the taps until the right temperature is reached. The plants will rot if they are watered to excess and an average of once a week in the summer and once every 10 days in the winter will be found a good working rule. If for some reason the temperature falls during the winter, you will want to keep the plants very much on the dry side, but the plants will receive quite a check during this period and will take some time to emerge from it.

In selecting plants to purchase you will find that the varieties that will do best in the home are those with dark leaves and thick flower stems, such as the various forms of Englert's 'Diana'. The light-coloured-leaved varieties are quite often more attractive to look at, but they are more liable to rot if their treatment is unsatisfactory; the dark-leaved forms are certainly best for the beginner. The possession of thick flower stems appears to indicate that the plants will be more generous in producing flowers, will hold these flowers for longer and will carry them upright, well above the foliage. Most of the single-flowered varieties tend to drop their flowers rather rapidly, but there are some strains which hold their flowers until they fade and this will occur with all the double-flowered types. The dead flowers should be cut off, as otherwise they may rot and cause rot to travel down the stem into the centre of the plant.

As far as African violets are concerned the plastic pot is certainly superior to the clay pot, the edges of which used to damage the leaf stalks and subsequently the plants. The plants will need no feeding during the year of purchase and only small quantities in ensuing years. They rarely require potting-on, but if this should be necessary a very thin light, open mixture is necessary, as they have very thin, weak roots. The recommended mixture is 3 parts peat, 1 part loam and 1 part grit. The plants should do well in soilless composts. They are one of the best flowering plants for bottle gardens, although they are not often seen in them.

Propagation is quite simple. A leaf with its stalk is inserted shallowly in the propagating medium in early spring and after three or four weeks you should find a number of small plant-lets developing at the base. These should be grown-on in some suitable compost and, as soon as they are large enough to handle, should be separated. In the nursery the tiny plantlets are pricked out in boxes, but in the home, they can probably be placed in one pot. As they get larger they can be given in-dividual 3-inch pots. The first flower spikes to appear should be pulled off, although this needs some strength of mind and it will take about a year for a good flowering plant to develop. If you do not separate the plantlets, you will get a large leafy plant that will be disinclined to flower well, and it is better to resort to the rather fiddling work of separating the plants. The point of taking the cuttings in early spring is that you have all the summer in which to establish these plantlets.

Although they are finicky enough in many ways, African violets do not seem to be much affected by gas or oil fumes and, provided that you can supply the necessary conditions, the presence of a gas fire or a paraffin heater should not deter you.

If you are successful with your saintpaulias you should have two or three flushes of flower each year, which is considerably more flower than you are likely to get from any other pot plant, so it is obviously worth while taking the additional trouble that these plants entail. You will be well rewarded.

Sansevieria trifasciata laurentii (Mother-in-law's Tongue) (I)

We are probably being too conservative in giving this plant an 'I' as it should do perfectly well under Cool conditions, provided it is kept very much on the dry side during the winter. There is no trouble in doing this, as the plant has very thick, tough, leathery leaves, a clear indication that it may have to tolerate periods of drought. Even during the spring and summer it will not require great quantities of water, although it should be provided in moderation when the condition of the soil calls for it.

The plant has erect leaves that are usually about 18 inches high in well-grown specimens, although greater heights have been recorded in the wild. These leaves are 2–3 inches across, and have a very thin green margin with a yellow stripe next to it, while the centre of the leaf is grey-green with transverse bands of a darker colour. The plant produces one fresh leaf each year. This is borne on the end of a rhizome, a creeping underground stem, and sometimes appears at some little distance from the main plant. It is tempting to sever the rhizome and get a fresh plant, but this should be done with some care, as it is some time after the leaf appears before roots start to form at the base. If, when the new leaf is about 8 inches high, you burrow down to find the rhizome and cut it about three-quarters through, you will encourage the formation of roots at the base of the new leaf. Once it is well rooted it is safe to sever the rhizome completely and pot-up the new leaf, which will produce fresh leaves in turn. It is also possible to cut a leaf and insert it in a propagating medium, when it will make roots. However, the leaves that appear subsequently from a leaf cutting like this will lack the yellow stripes and be a plain, mottled green; handsome enough, but less so than the variegated forms.

The plant requires a well-lit situation, although it seems to tolerate quite shady conditions as well. Gas and oil fumes are shrugged off as of no account and the plant presents few difficulties, so long as it is not overwatered. As a general rule a watering each month is sufficient in the winter and even in the summer you will not have to water very frequently. The plants are somewhat greedy and like a rather heavy compost and it does not seem very likely that soilless composts would prove very suitable.

Schefflera actinophylla (I)

Until about 20 years ago, schefflera was a very obscure genus and few botanists, let alone gardeners, were at all familiar with the plants in it. Then it was found that they made very ornamental house-plants and they became extremely popular. Indeed, they have now become popular for long enough for plants to have flowered in cultivation, with the result that it has been shown that the plants are not, in point of fact, scheffleras, but belong to a related genus, *Brassaia*. However, they have been known so long as scheffleras that they will probably keep the name.

Although they can eventually make quite sizeable trees, the plants are slow-growing. As they increase in size they also produce larger leaves and a good-sized plant is considerably more handsome than the rather small specimen that is generally offered for sale. This is a plant that will improve every year and is best regarded as a long-term investment. The large leaves are composed of a number of elliptic leaflets, not unlike a monster horse-chestnut leaf. The number of these leaflets increases as the plant ages. In very young plants there are only three; medium-sized plants have the leaf composed of five leaflets, and older plants may have as many as ten. Each leaflet may reach a length of 10 inches so that a well-grown plant will have leaves 20 inches across. These leaflets radiate around the stalk like the rays of a light.

The plant likes Intermediate conditions and either a well-lit situation or partial shade; deep shade is resented. Although the atmosphere should never be too dry, this plant does not insist on the very moist atmospheres that are required, for example, by calatheas or African violets. The compost should be fairly rich and the plant should be regularly fed in the growing season. It should not dry out at any time and should be potted-on whenever it becomes pot-bound. This probably means a yearly potting-on until it has got into a fairly large pot. Since your object is to get a large specimen as soon as possible, this is all to the good. If your house cannot accommodate a large plant, there is not much point in purchasing a schefflera in the first place. If you have a position where a large plant will be suitable, there are few more fascinating plants than this; it is extremely interesting to see the plant improve yearly.

It is not the sort of plant that one would imagine a soilless compost would suit, but such composts have not really been in use long enough for us to find out how they respond to plants that will remain in the same soil for long periods.

101

Schefflera's reaction to gas and oil fumes is tolerant but not enthusiastic.

Scindapsus aureus (I)

This plant, which requires treatment similar to that recommended for *Philodendron scandens* also resembles that plant in many ways. Indeed, it might be said that scindapsus is to East Asia what philodendron is to South America, although there are fewer species of scindapsus. The leaves are less markedly heart-shaped and come to a finer point, but are of about the same dimensions. They are dark green flecked with yellow. The variety known as 'Golden Queen' has considerably more yellow on the leaves than the type, while in the variety 'Silver Queen', the leaf is mainly white in colour.

A moist atmosphere and a well-lit but shaded situation are what this plant requires and it resents gas or oil fumes. If the situation is too dark, you will not see the yellow markings develop on the leaf, although the plant will grow quite satisfactorily. In any case leaves produced during the winter months are liable to be of a poor colour and the section of stem bearing small or badly coloured leaves can be removed at the beginning of April, with the assurance that the plant will break again and produce respectable leaves. The plant will survive under Cool conditions, but must then be kept as dry as possible during the winter. At all times watering should be controlled as excess leads to the leaves browning round the edges and, eventually, to the plant rotting. During the summer in warm weather a syringe can be employed with great advantage and the plant seems to take as much water through the leaves as it does from the soil.

Senecio macroglossus variegatus (German Ivy, Cape Ivy) (C, I)

This climber belongs to the same genus as the common groundsel (and the gaudy cineraria), and comes from South Africa. It is a twining plant with leaves that are very similar to those of the ivy, being roughly triangular, shallowly 5- or 7-lobed and up to 2½ inches long and as much across. The variegated form has a cream margin. Once the plant has reached a sufficient height it will bear quite large yellow daisies and tends to do this in the autumn and winter. The leaves are rather fleshy and, apart from the routine sponging, should be kept free of water. The plant itself never requires great quantities of water, but does not relish drying out. A light position is needed and a dry atmosphere is not resented. Gas and oil fumes are liable to cause damage and the plant is not suitable where these forms of heating are used.

Planted out in a greenhouse or conservatory border the plant will grow very rapidly, but it is more restrained in a pot in the home. It is, however, somewhat greedy and needs ample feeding during the summer. Pinching-out the growing points in spring will encourage the production of side-shoots and a good bushy plant, but if you hope to produce flowers you should let it climb unstopped. It will, however, have practically reached ceiling height before flowers are produced and it is not every room that this sort of growth will suit. In any case the shining, waxy leaves are the plant's main attractions. Cuttings of half-ripe wood will root fairly readily.

Spathiphyllum wallisii (White Sails) (I, W)

This member of the arum family is grown for the sake of its flowers. These are produced in the spring and, sometimes, again in the autumn. The leaves are lance-shaped, coming to a sharp point, about 4 inches long and a bright shining green. The flowers are composed of a white spathe, which fades to pale green as it ages, and which surrounds the spadix, the club-like process which most of the arum family show and on which the true flowers are borne. These are small and inconspicuous.

The plant is remarkably greedy and can scarcely be overfed, and will need repotting yearly. During the summer it will require plenty of water and should not be allowed to dry out, even in the winter. It dislikes gas and oil fumes, but is not killed by them. It requires a shady position and will do well in quite dark situations, although this can be overdone. It is very susceptible to attacks by the red spider mite, so that a damp atmosphere is essential and frequent sprayings an advantage. The plant increases in size fairly rapidly and can be divided in the spring, when flowering is completed, so that more plants are easy to obtain. When dividing the plant, care must be taken not to damage the roots more than necessary; it is very difficult to avoid some damage. Provided its essential requirements are met, this is by no means a difficult plant. The flowers remain attractive for about four weeks, so they earn their rent and the leaves, although plain green, are also attractive with their shining surface.

Tradescantia (Wandering Jew) (C)

This genus includes, together with zebrina, the easiest of all house-plants to grow. They seem to be indifferent as to soil, to position or to temperature, provided they are kept frost-free, and they are very easy to propagate. Although they are so easy to grow, they are not particularly easy to refer to their respective species.

Tradescantia 'Rochford's Quicksilver'

This has quite long leaves that are an elongated oval in shape and bright emerald green in colour with conspicuous silver stripes. It is probably a form of *T. elongata* and requires slightly warmer conditions than the other species to be discussed. Even so it will thrive under Cool conditions. During the summer, growth is very rapid and the plant will need stopping once or twice. All the tradescantias like to be fairly moist, and they will survive treatment that would be fatal to most other plants. The plant does best in a well-lit situation, but does not like direct sunlight. Like all tradescantias, if portions of the plant are inserted in water, they will soon produce roots. It is easier, however, to put seven small cuttings in a 3-inch pot: five around the edge and two in the centre. They are very brittle and must be inserted with care in a rather light compost. Soilless composts should suit them admirably. These cuttings should either be watered in with a fine rose fitted to the watering-can, or alternatively the pot should be stood in water, so that the water ascends from below. If this is not done, there is a risk that the cuttings may be washed out of the soil. This form of watering should be persisted in for two or three weeks, until the cuttings are rooted. They will quickly grow away and make a respectable potful in a very short time. All these variegated tradescantias, with the exception of 'Rochford's Quicksilver', are liable to throw shoots that have plain green leaves. These should be removed as soon as detected, as otherwise they will take the plant over. All the varieties will tend to hang if placed in a suitable position. Sometimes you will produce a plant with attractive trails but a rather bare centre; if this occurs you can insert a couple of cuttings in the centre and they will clothe the bare portion.

Tradescantia 'Silver'

This has rather small leaves, oval in shape and about 2 inches long and 1 inch across and is variegated with white streaks that may be minimal or may cover most of the surface. If placed in a sunlit place and kept rather dry, the whole plant will be suffused with pink, although this is compensated for by slower growth and smaller leaves. Otherwise it will do best in a well-lit situation that is not exposed to much direct sunshine. As the leaves spring directly from the stem, this is probably a form of *T. albiflora*.

Tradescantia 'Tricolor'

In this variety the leaves are slightly larger than in the 'silver' tradescantia and have rather narrower stripes of white, pink and yellowish-cream. It will also grow in rather shadier situations. The leaves are attached to the trailing stems by very short stalks, which suggests that it is a form of *T. fluminensis*, but it is by no means easy to distinguish *T. fluminensis* and *T. albiflora*, although the presence or absence of a leaf stalk is one of the differentiating features.

Although they will grow perfectly happily in bottle gardens, the tradescantias are not really very suitable for these, as they grow so vigorously they are liable to swamp any other plants. They are also so easy to grow in the ordinary way that it seems rather a waste to put them in the bottle.

Vriesia splendens (I)

Another of the epiphytic bromeliads, requiring treatment similar to aechmea and neoregelia. The sword-shaped leaves will reach a foot in length and are 3 inches across, while the rosette is about 19 inches across and a foot high. The leaves are dark green with maroon-coloured transverse bands. When the flower stem starts to emerge, these maroon bands gradually disappear. The flower stem is some 8 inches high, but the actual inflorescence is sometimes as much as 15 inches long and 1½ inches across. It is composed of bright scarlet bracts, that overlap each other and from which short-lived yellow flowers emerge. These bracts retain their colour for at least eight weeks and so give very good value for money, quite apart from the fact that the banded leaves are very handsome in their own right.

The plant does best in a well-lit situation, but not one in direct sunlight, although this is not liable to do much harm in this country. The vase should be kept full of water and rain-water is preferable if it can be collected. It should be of room temperature when applied. Although Intermediate temperatures are best, the plant will survive under Cool conditions, although it will grow more slowly and the tips of the leaves are liable to wither during the winter. A temperature of 45°F is rather low, but if you can supply a constant 50°F, you need have no hesitation in growing this plant.

Zebrina pendula (C)

Zebrina has been separated from the genus *Tradescantia* owing to the different shape of the flowers, but the plants are very similar in appearance, need much the same treatment and are equally easy to propagate. The leaves are attached to the stems by a short stalk and are oval in shape, up to 3 inches long and 1½ inches across. They have a very narrow dark green margin, two lateral zones of silvery-grey and a broad dark green central band. The underside of the leaf is purple, and it is well worth placing the plant above eye level because of this so that the contrasting colours of the upper and lower sides can be enjoyed. If the plant is kept on the dry side (but this should never be overdone) the purple colour is enhanced. The plant likes a semi-shady position; too much light turns the purple an unpleasing rusty-brown.

There is a very attractive variety, *Zebrina pendula quadricolor*, which is by no means so easy to grow as the type. In this variety the leaves are striped white, purple, silvery-green and dark green. It needs to be kept on the dry side, as it rots easily and to be given the most brightly-lit situation you can provide. In shade the variegation vanishes. In any case any leaves produced during the winter will lack this variegation, but if these unvariegated leaves are removed during the early spring, the succeeding leaves will be of the required colour. This variety appreciates warmth and might do better under Intermediate conditions. Although the leaves are quite spectacular, the variety is not so satisfactory a house-plant as the type.

With zebrina we come to the end of our list. There are, of course, many other house-plants grown, but we think we have listed the easiest and the most popular. If you are only starting your collection of house-plants, we hope you will find in the list descriptions of plants that will fill your needs. There really are plants to suit every position and every house. Growing plants is one of the most satisfying of occupations and we hope you will enjoy it.

APPENDIX I

QUICK REFERENCE LISTS OF HOUSE-PLANTS FOR BEGINNERS

GENERAL

Araucaria excelsa
Cissus antarctica
Chlorophytum comosum variegatum
X *Fatshedera lizei*
Fatsia japonica
Ficus elastica decora
Hedera canariensis

Hedera helix
Neanthe bella
Philodendron scandens
Pilea cadierei nana
Rhoicissus rhomboidea
Tradescantia spp.
Zebrina pendula

FOR SHADY POSITIONS

Asplenium nidus
Begonia spp.
Calathea spp.
Ficus pumila
Hedera spp. with unvariegated leaves

Maranta spp.
Philodendron scandens
Tradescantia spp.
Zebrina spp.

108

WITH ATTRACTIVE FLOWERS

Aechmea rhodocyanea
Aphelandra squarrosa louisae
Beloperone guttata
Hypocyrta glabra
Impatiens petersiana

Peperomia caperata
Peperomia hederaefolia
Senecio macroglossus
variegatus
Vriesia splendens

APPENDIX II
TEMPERATURE CONVERSION TABLE
for degrees Fahrenheit to degrees Celsius

°F	°C	°F	°C	°F	°C
32	0·0	55	12·8	78	25·6
33	0·6	56	13·3	79	26·1
34	1·1	57	13·9	80	26·7
35	1·7	58	14·4	81	27·2
36	2·2	59	15·0	82	27·8
37	2·8	60	15·6	83	28·3
38	3·3	61	16·1	84	28·9
39	3·9	62	16·7	85	29·4
40	4·4	63	17·2	86	30·0
41	5·0	64	17·8	87	30·6
42	5·6	65	18·3	88	31·1
43	6·1	66	18·9	89	31·7
44	6·7	67	19·4	90	32·2
45	7·2	68	20·0	91	32·8
46	7·8	69	20·6	92	33·3
47	8·3	70	21·1	93	33·9
48	8·9	71	21·7	94	34·4
49	9·4	72	22·2	95	35·0
50	10·0	73	22·8	96	35·6
51	10·6	74	23·3	97	36·1
52	11·1	75	23·9	98	36·7
53	11·7	76	24·4	99	37·2
54	12·2	77	25·5	100	37·8

INDEX

Figures in bold type are plate numbers